SIX SISTERS' STUFF

30-Minute Meals

Other Cookbooks by
SIX SISTERS' STUFF

Celebrate Every Season

Copycat Cooking

Dinner Made Easy

Healthy Eats

Instant Cooking

Six Ingredients

Six Sisters' Stuff

Sweets and Treats

12 Days of Christmas

A Year with Six Sisters' Stuff

SIX SISTERS' STUFF

30-Minute Meals

SHADOW
MOUNTAIN
PUBLISHING

To the ones who plan, cook, and serve dinner—day after day after day—
we hope this makes your life just a little bit easier.

Photography: Michele Lee
Food prep and styling assistant: Megan Jessop

Library of Congress Cataloging-in-Publication Data

Names: Six Sisters' Stuff, issuing body.
Title: 30-minute meals / Six Sisters' Stuff.
Other titles: 30-minute meals (Shadow Mountain Publishing) | Thirty-minute meals
Description: [Salt Lake City, Utah] : Shadow Mountain Publishing, [2025] | Includes index. | Summary: "Six Sisters' Stuff returns with a cookbook featuring delicious recipes that can be made in 30 minutes"—Provided by publisher.
Identifiers: LCCN 2024060390 (print) | LCCN 2024060391 (ebook) | ISBN 9781639934263 (trade paperback) | ISBN 9781649334589 (ebook)
Subjects: LCSH: Quick and easy cooking. | LCGFT: Cookbooks.
Classification: LCC TX833.5 .A138 2025 (print) | LCC TX833.5 (ebook) | DDC 641.5/12—dc23/eng/20250131
LC record available at https://lccn.loc.gov/2024060390
LC ebook record available at https://lccn.loc.gov/2024060391

Printed in China
Regent Publishing Services Limited, Hong Kong, China

10 9 8 7 6 5 4 3 2 1

Contents

APPETIZERS | 1

BEEF DISHES | 25

CHICKEN DISHES | 49

MEATLESS DISHES | 77

PORK DISHES | 93

SEAFOOD DISHES | 119

TURKEY DISHES | 137

SIDE DISHES | 157

DESSERTS | 199

INDEX | 224

Appetizers

Air Fryer Parmesan Spinach
  Stuffed Mushrooms 2

Bacon-Wrapped Tater Tots
  with Dipping Sauce 5

Buffalo Ranch Deviled Eggs 6

Chicken Taco Roll-Ups 8

Twisted Pretzel Bites 11

Zucchini Feta Bruschetta 12

DIPS
Green Goddess
  Vegetable Dip 15

Million-Dollar Dip 17

Multicooker Spinach
  Artichoke Dip 18

Queso Blanco Dip 21

Warm Bacon Cheese Dip 23

Air Fryer Parmesan Spinach Stuffed Mushrooms

These cook in just 10 minutes, but taste like you put a lot more effort into them. Filled with spinach, stuffing, and two types of cheese, these will be gone before you can blink.

Prep time: 10 min | Cook time: 10 min | Total time: 20 min | Makes about 35 mushrooms

---

1½ cups hot water

1 (6-ounce) package chicken flavor stuffing mix, such as Stove Top

2 pounds fresh mushrooms, whole

2 tablespoons butter

2 cloves garlic, minced

1 cup chopped spinach

1 cup shredded mozzarella cheese

1 cup grated Parmesan cheese

Nonstick cooking spray

1. In a large bowl, mix hot water and stuffing mix together. Stir until moistened. Set aside.
2. Remove stems from mushroom caps. Set caps aside and chop stems. Melt butter in a skillet on medium heat. Add chopped stems and garlic. Cook and stir for 5 minutes or until tender.
3. Add garlic mushroom stems to the stuffing mixture along with the spinach and cheeses. Mix well. Spoon into the mushroom caps.
4. Spray the air fryer basket with cooking spray and place filled mushroom caps inside. Depending on the size of your air fryer, you may need to work in batches.
5. Cook at 350 degrees F. about 10 minutes. The mushroom caps should be dark brown and the cheese and stuffing should be slightly golden.

Bacon-Wrapped Tater Tots with Dipping Sauce

The ultimate crowd-pleaser, these crispy-on-the-outside, soft-on-the-inside tots are a perfect bite-size treat that disappears in no time. Don't forget the sauce!

Prep time: 10 min | Cook time: 20 min | Total time: 30 min | Makes about 40 tots

TATER TOTS

1 (32-ounce package) tater tots, thawed to room temperature

1 (16-ounce) package bacon

Toothpicks

⅓ cup brown sugar

¼ teaspoon chili powder

SAUCE

½ cup mayonnaise

2 tablespoons ketchup

1 tablespoon horseradish

⅓ teaspoon paprika

¼ teaspoon salt

⅛ teaspoon oregano

Pinch black pepper

½ teaspoon cayenne pepper hot sauce, such as Frank's RedHot

1. Preheat oven to 400 degrees F. Cover a half-sheet baking pan with foil or parchment paper.
2. Cut each bacon strip into thirds and wrap one piece around a tater tot. Use a toothpick to secure the bacon to the tot. Repeat until all the bacon has been used.
3. Combine the brown sugar and chili powder in a small bowl. Roll each bacon-wrapped tot in the brown sugar mixture. Place on prepared baking pan seam side down. Repeat for each tot, placing them close together but not touching.
4. Bake tots for 10 minutes. Remove from oven and turn each tot over, seam side up, then bake 10 more minutes or until the bacon is crispy.
5. For the sauce, mix all ingredients together and refrigerate until ready to serve.

Buffalo Ranch Deviled Eggs

A fun twist on a classic appetizer, these deviled eggs have the perfect balance of spicy and creamy.

Prep time: 10 min | Total time: 10 min | Makes 24 appetizers

---

12 eggs, hard-boiled

1 tablespoon buffalo sauce, such as Frank's Red Hot Buffalo Sauce

1½ tablespoons liquid ranch dressing

2 green onions, chopped

1 tablespoon crumbled feta cheese

1. Peel and halve the eggs.
2. Separate the yolks and place them together in a bowl. Mash the yolks with a fork until no chunks remain.
3. Add in the buffalo sauce and ranch dressing and mix until smooth.
4. Scoop 1–2 teaspoons of yolk mixture into each egg white half.
5. Top with green onions, feta cheese, and more buffalo sauce if desired.

Chicken Taco Roll-Ups

This no-bake appetizer works great with leftover chicken or rotisserie chicken. Dipped in salsa, these roll-ups make a great snack or even a light lunch.

Prep time: 10 min | Total time: 10 min | Makes 40 roll-ups

3 cups shredded chicken

1 (8-ounce) package fat-free cream cheese

1 cup shredded Mexican cheese blend

⅓ cup salsa

4 green onions, chopped

½ avocado, diced

2 tablespoons taco seasoning

1 teaspoon garlic

1 teaspoon garlic salt

Salt and pepper, to taste

4 (10-inch) flour tortillas

1. In a large bowl, mix together the shredded chicken, cream cheese, Mexican cheese, salsa, and onions with a hand mixer.
2. Add the diced avocado, taco seasoning, garlic, garlic salt, salt, and pepper, and mix at a slow speed.
3. Spread a thin layer over a tortilla and roll up the tortilla.
4. Cut into 1-inch bites. Repeat with each tortilla.
5. Refrigerate until ready to serve.

Twisted Pretzel Bites

Who knew making pretzels at home could be so easy? We love these served with Queso Blanco Dip (see recipe on page 21), a flavored cream cheese, or even a hazelnut spread.

Prep time: 15 min | Cook time: 12 min | Total time: 27 min | Makes 18 pretzel bites

Nonstick cooking spray

Flour (enough to lightly flour surface)

1 (13.8-ounce) tube refrigerated pizza crust

5 cups water

⅓ cup baking soda

1 egg, slightly beaten

2 teaspoons coarse kosher salt

1. Preheat oven to 450 degrees F.
2. Spray half-sheet baking pan with nonstick cooking spray.
3. Unroll dough on a lightly floured surface.
4. Cut the dough into 3 ½-inch strips. Using your hands, roll each strip into a rope about 5 inches long.
5. Tie each strip into a knot and place on the baking sheet.
6. In a large saucepan, bring water and baking soda to a boil.
7. Drop dough knots, 6 at a time, into the boiling water.
8. Let the knots cook for about 30 seconds or until the dough looks slightly puffy and dimpled.
9. Using a slotted spoon, remove knots from the water and place on the cookie sheet about ½ inch apart.
10. Brush knots with egg and sprinkle on salt.
11. Bake for 10 to 12 minutes or until well browned.
12. Serve pretzel bites with your favorite dip.

Zucchini Feta Bruschetta

The ultimate summer appetizer with light lemon and olive flavors mixed with fresh herbs and summer produce, all piled on top of a toasted piece of crusty bread.

Prep time: 15 min | Cook time: 6 min | Total time: 21 min | Makes about 24 appetizers

---

1 crusty baguette cut on a diagonal into 1-inch slices

⅓ cup olive oil

2 zucchini, sliced paper-thin using a mandoline

2 tablespoons olive oil

2 teaspoons lemon juice

1 teaspoon lemon zest

2 tablespoons minced shallot

2 garlic cloves, minced

¼ teaspoon red chili pepper flakes

¾ cup crumbled feta cheese

¼ cup chopped fresh basil

Salt and pepper, to taste

1. Preheat the oven to 400 degrees F. and line a baking sheet with parchment paper.
2. Brush both sides of each slice of bread with olive oil and arrange the slices on the prepared baking sheet. Bake for 3 minutes, flip, and bake for an additional 3 minutes.
3. In a large mixing bowl, gently toss together the zucchini, olive oil, lemon juice, lemon zest, shallot, garlic, chili flakes, feta, and basil. Taste the zucchini topping and season with salt and pepper as desired.
4. Top each piece of toasted baguette with a couple of tablespoons of zucchini topping.

Green Goddess Vegetable Dip

Fresh and light, this dip is bursting with herbs and tangy flavors. It pairs great with your favorite veggies or pita bread.

Prep time: 10 min | Total time: 10 min | Makes about 3 cups

---

1 cup sour cream

1 cup mayonnaise

⅓ cup fresh parsley leaves

⅓ cup fresh dill

⅓ cup fresh basil leaves

1 tablespoon lemon juice

1 tablespoon lime juice

2 teaspoons minced garlic

2 green onions, diced

½ cup crumbled feta cheese

½ cup olive oil

Salt, to taste

1. Place all ingredients in a blender or food processor.

2. Mix until completely smooth.

3. Serve with fresh vegetables or pita bread. Store any leftovers in the refrigerator for up to one week.

Million-Dollar Dip

We imagine this dip tastes like scoring the winning touchdown. Its creamy base, bacon, and slivered almonds for a crunch, means you can't eat just one bite.

Prep time: 15 min | Total time: 15 min | Makes about 3 cups

6 ounces cream cheese, softened

⅓ cup sour cream

½ cup mayonnaise

1 cup shredded sharp cheddar cheese

1 cup shredded pepper jack cheese

10 slices thick-cut bacon, cooked and crumbled

3 green onions, sliced

1 teaspoon sea salt

½ teaspoon ground black pepper

½ teaspoon garlic powder

¼ teaspoon onion powder

½ cup toasted slivered almonds

Snack crackers such as Ritz or Club, for serving

1. Using a hand mixer or stand mixer, beat the cream cheese on high speed for about 2 minutes.
2. Decrease the mixing speed to low and add the sour cream and mayonnaise and mix until smooth.
3. Add the cheeses, bacon, green onions, sea salt, ground black pepper, garlic powder, onion powder, and toasted slivered almonds and mix until combined.
4. Serve with snack crackers, such as Ritz or Club.

Multicooker Spinach Artichoke Dip

Make this classic appetizer even easier by using your multicooker, and it will keep warm nicely until you're ready to serve.

Prep time: 5 min | Cook time: 4 min | Pressurize time: 10 min | Total time: 19 min | Serves 10

1 (10-ounce) package fresh baby spinach, roughly chopped

1 (14-ounce) jar canned artichoke hearts, drained and roughly chopped

½ cup sour cream

½ cup mayonnaise

½ cup chopped onion

2 cloves garlic, minced

½ teaspoon garlic salt

1 (8-ounce) package cream cheese, cut into pieces

½ cup chicken broth

2 cups shredded Parmesan cheese

2 cups shredded mozzarella cheese

Salt and pepper, to taste

1. Add spinach, artichoke hearts, sour cream, mayonnaise, onion, garlic, garlic salt, and cream cheese to the bottom of the multicooker. Mix all together. Pour the chicken broth over everything.
2. Place the lid on and secure it in place. Turn the vent to SEAL (if not automatic) and cook for 4 minutes.
3. When the cooking is finished, move the knob to VENT and do a quick release of the pressure.
4. Remove the lid and add in the Parmesan and mozzarella cheeses; mix until everything is incorporated. Season with salt and pepper to taste.
5. Keep on a warm setting until ready to serve with crackers, bread, or vegetables.

Queso Blanco Dip

Creamy white American cheese, green chiles, and jalapeño combine to make a flavorful queso dip that will have everyone asking for the recipe.

Prep time: 10 min | Total time: 10 min | Serves 10

1¼ pounds white American cheese, cut into 1-inch cubes

1 (4-ounce) can diced green chiles

2 jalapeños, seeded and diced

⅔ cup half-and-half

½ cup cold water

1. Place all ingredients into a microwave-safe bowl.
2. Microwave on high for 5 minutes, stopping to stir after every minute. It might appear runny at first, but it will thicken up as it begins to cool down.
3. Serve immediately with tortilla chips.

Warm Bacon Cheese Dip

This dip is loaded with thick bacon, three types of cheese, and baked to perfection. It tastes great with crackers, bread, or veggies.

Prep time: 10 min | Cook time: 10 min | Total time: 20 min | Serves 8

Nonstick cooking spray

8 strips thick-cut bacon, divided

1 (8-ounce) package cream cheese, softened

1 cup shredded cheddar cheese

1 cup shredded Parmesan cheese

⅓ cup mayonnaise

3 green onions, thinly sliced, divided

1 teaspoon garlic powder

½ teaspoon onion powder

1. Preheat the oven to 350 degrees F. Spray an 8x8 baking pan with nonstick cooking spray.
2. Cook 8 strips of bacon to desired crispiness. Crumble 6 strips and set aside the other 2 strips for later.
3. In a medium bowl, mix together crumbled bacon, cream cheese, cheddar cheese, Parmesan cheese, mayonnaise, 2 green onions, garlic powder, and onion powder.
4. Spread the mixture in prepared 8x8 pan and cook for 10 minutes, then stir. Crumble the two remaining bacon strips and top the bacon-cheese mixture with the bacon crumbles and remaining green onion. Cook for 5 more minutes, then remove from oven and serve with crackers, bread, chips, or vegetables.

Beef Dishes

Air Fryer Cube Steak
with Gravy. 26

Asian-Inspired Beef and
Snow Peas. 29

BBQ Sloppy Joes 30

Chopped Cheese Sandwich 33

Classic Burgers 34

Creamy Beef and
Tomato Pasta 36

Fiesta Ground Beef
Enchiladas 39

Grilled Teriyaki Burgers 41

Ground Beef Quesadillas 42

Multicooker Ravioli
Lasagna Soup 45

Oven-Baked Beef Tacos. 46

Air Fryer Cube Steak with Gravy

Breaded, juicy steak pieces that pair perfectly with a homemade brown gravy for a home run meal.

Prep time: 10 min | Cook time: 10 min | Total time: 20 min | Serves 4

CUBE STEAK

2 pounds cube steak, divided into
  4 equal portions

2 teaspoons salt

1 teaspoon ground black pepper

3 eggs

2 tablespoons buttermilk

1 cup flour

1 cup seasoned breadcrumbs

GRAVY

3 tablespoons butter

3 tablespoons flour

1½ cups milk

Salt and pepper, to taste

1. Lay the cube steak pieces flat on a cutting board and cover them with plastic wrap. Use a meat mallet or a rolling pin to flatten each piece to an even thickness (about ⅓ inch).
2. Season each piece of cube steak on both sides with salt and pepper.
3. Whisk the eggs and buttermilk together in a shallow bowl or pie pan large enough to dip the steak into. Put the flour in another bowl or pie pan and the breadcrumbs in a third bowl or pie pan. Line the bowls up in the following order: flour, egg mixture, breadcrumbs.
4. Preheat the air fryer to 425 degrees F.
5. Dip a piece of cube steak in the flour and flip to coat both sides. Next, dip it in the egg mixture, coating both sides. Finally, dip the cube steak in the breadcrumbs, coating both sides. Repeat with the remaining steaks.
6. Arrange the breaded steaks in a single layer in the basket of the preheated air fryer. Don't crowd the air fryer. If you have to cook in batches, do so. Fry for 5 minutes on each side.
7. While the steak is cooking, make the gravy. Melt the butter over medium heat in a saucepan. Once

melted, whisk in the flour and cook until smooth and bubbling slightly, whisking continuously. Slowly add the milk, ½ cup at a time, stirring continuously. Let the mixture simmer for a couple of minutes or until thickened to your liking. You can add more milk if you prefer a thinner gravy. Season with salt and pepper to taste.

8. Serve the cube steak warm, doused in gravy.

Asian-Inspired Beef and Snow Peas

Make a fresh, healthier version of your favorite takeout at home with this delicious seasoned beef with fresh snow peas.

Prep time: 10 min | Cook time: 10 min | Total time: 20 min | Serves 4

BEEF

2 tablespoons extra virgin olive oil

1½ cups sliced mushrooms

1 pound beef sirloin, sliced into thin strips

5 ounces snow peas

1 cup chopped kale

2 cups cooked brown rice

SAUCE

½ cup soy sauce

4 tablespoons brown sugar

2 tablespoons rice vinegar

½ teaspoon ginger

1 tablespoon hoisin sauce

4 garlic cloves, minced

1. In a skillet over medium heat, combine the oil and mushrooms. Stir occasionally and sauté for 5 minutes.
2. While mushrooms are cooking, start making the sauce by combining all sauce ingredients in a bowl and whisking until combined.
3. After the mushrooms have cooked, add the beef to the skillet and continue flipping occasionally until beef is browned on both sides.
4. Add snow peas and kale to skillet, then slowly pour sauce over the whole skillet.
5. Reduce heat to low and allow sauce to heat up while stirring occasionally for 2 minutes.
6. Serve over brown rice.

BBQ Sloppy Joes

Not your average sloppy joe recipe! This one is loaded with BBQ sauce, tasty green peppers, lean ground beef, and diced onions that the whole family will love.

Prep time: 5 min | Cook time: 10 min | Total time: 15 min | Serves 6

1 pound 80/20 or 85/15 lean ground beef or ground turkey

½ cup diced onion

1 green pepper, diced

1 cup barbeque sauce, such as Sweet Baby Ray's

Salt and pepper, to taste

6 hamburger buns

1. Brown meat in a saucepan over medium heat.
2. After meat is almost cooked through, add onion and green pepper and sauté for 5 minutes or until vegetables are soft.
3. Add barbecue sauce and warm on stovetop until heated through. Season with salt and pepper, as desired.
4. Serve on hamburger buns.

Chopped Cheese Sandwich

Our budget-friendly version of a classic New York–style chopped cheese sandwich makes the perfect weeknight dinner.

Prep time: 5 min | Cook time: 20 min | Total time: 25 min | Serves 4

4 hoagie rolls

2 tablespoons butter, divided

1 onion, diced

1 pound ground beef

1 teaspoon salt

½ teaspoon ground black pepper

½ teaspoon garlic powder

8 slices American cheese

Mayonnaise, to taste

Ketchup, to taste

Shredded lettuce, optional

Tomatoes, optional

1. Slice hoagie rolls open.
2. Heat a large skillet over medium-high heat and add 1 tablespoon butter. Once the butter is melted, place the hoagies on the skillet so that the inside surface gets toasted, about 2–3 minutes. Set toasted buns aside.
3. Add remaining butter to pan and sauté onions until they are translucent, about 3 minutes. Push onions to the side of the pan and add ground beef as one large patty. Let the ground beef start to brown without breaking it up, letting it sear for 3–4 minutes. Season with salt, pepper, and garlic powder and then flip the large ground beef patty over to sear the other side, about 2–3 minutes.
4. Start to chop up the ground beef using a spatula or ChopStir and work the onions in with the beef. Continue to chop and cook the beef until no pink remains, about 3 minutes. Divide the meat into 4 even portions and top each portion with 2 slices of cheese. Allow the cheese to melt while in the skillet.
5. Spread mayonnaise and ketchup on the inside of the buns, then top with beef and cheese mixture. Add other preferred toppings, such as tomatoes and lettuce, and then serve.

Classic Burgers

The hunt for the go-to homemade burger recipe is over with these classic patties that turn out the perfect barbecue staple every time.

Prep time: 15 min | Cook time: 10 min | Total time: 25 min | Serves 8

PATTIES

2 pounds 85/15 lean ground beef

1 egg, beaten

¾ cup breadcrumbs

3 tablespoons evaporated milk

2 tablespoons Worcestershire sauce

2 cloves garlic, minced

1 teaspoon salt

1 teaspoon garlic powder

1 teaspoon onion powder

Dash of cayenne pepper

BURGERS

8 hamburger buns

8 slices cheddar cheese

Lettuce, for topping

Tomatoes, for topping

Pickles, for topping

Sliced red onion, for topping

1. For patties, in a large mixing bowl, add all ingredients. Mix together using your hands until ingredients are barely combined. Do not overmix, because then the hamburgers will become dense.
2. Form the mixture into 8 patties. Make them a little larger than the hamburger buns that you plan to use because ground beef shrinks as it cooks.
3. Preheat the grill to medium-high heat.
4. Lightly oil the grill grate and place patties on the grill.
5. Grill patties until no longer pink on the inside, or until they reach desired doneness, usually about 5 minutes on each side.
6. Place cooked burger on a toasted hamburger bun and top with favorite toppings.

Creamy Beef and Tomato Pasta

This delicious, comfort food pasta is one you'll keep coming back for time and time again.

Prep time: 15 min | Cook time: 15 min | Total time: 30 min | Serves 6

---

1 (12-ounce) package penne pasta

1 pound ground beef

1 medium onion, diced

3 cloves garlic, minced

1 (14.5-ounce) can Italian-style diced tomatoes

1 (8-ounce) can tomato sauce

1 cup half-and-half

½ teaspoon dried basil

¼ cup grated Parmesan cheese, for topping

Fresh chopped basil, optional garnish

1. Cook the pasta in salted water according to package directions until al dente.
2. While pasta is cooking, brown the ground beef and drain grease.
3. Add the onions and garlic to the beef and sauté for about 2 minutes.
4. Pour in the entire can of diced tomatoes and the can of tomato sauce and heat through.
5. Pour in the half-and-half and heat through. The longer you cook the sauce, the thicker it will get, so simmer it until it is the consistency you want.
6. Add the basil and let it simmer for a few minutes.
7. Drain the pasta and mix in the beef sauce.
8. Top each serving with a sprinkle of Parmesan cheese and fresh basil, if desired.

Fiesta Ground Beef Enchiladas

These enchiladas feel like a shortcut! Quickly throw together beef, beans, and corn, then top with cheese to make a scrumptious, filling dish everyone will love.

Prep time: 5 min | Cook time: 25 min | Total time: 30 min | Serves 8

---

1 (19-ounce) can red enchilada sauce, divided

1 pound lean ground beef

1 (15-ounce) can black beans, drained and rinsed

1 (15.25-ounce) can corn, drained

8 large flour tortillas

2 cups shredded Mexican cheese blend, divided

Favorite enchilada toppings, such as olives, lettuce, sour cream, guacamole, and tomatoes

1. Preheat the oven to 350 degrees F. Spread ½ cup of enchilada sauce in the bottom of a 9x13 baking pan.
2. In a skillet over medium heat, brown the ground beef. Drain, then stir in black beans and corn.
3. In each tortilla, spread an even amount of the ground beef mixture, along with 2 tablespoons of cheese. Roll up each tortilla and place it seam side down in the prepared baking dish.
4. Pour the remainder of the enchilada sauce over the top of the enchiladas and top with the remaining cheese.
5. Bake in the oven for 15–20 minutes, or until the edges start to brown, and the enchiladas are heated through.
6. Remove from the oven and serve with your favorite enchilada toppings.

Grilled Teriyaki Burgers

A sweet teriyaki sauce and pineapple flavor produces wonderfully juicy burger patties, topped with pineapple slices to make for a great Hawaiian-inspired burger.

Prep time: 5 min | Cook time: 25 min | Total time: 30 min | Serves 4

1 tablespoon olive oil

2 onions, thinly sliced

3 teaspoons sea salt, divided

1½ pounds 80/20 lean ground beef

1 teaspoon ground black pepper

9½ tablespoons teriyaki sauce, divided, such as Kikkoman or San-J

4 pineapple rings

4 hamburger buns, toasted

1. Heat the olive oil over medium-high heat in a medium heavy-bottomed skillet. Add the onions, season with 1 teaspoon sea salt, and sauté for 15 minutes until soft and golden brown, adding water as needed to keep the onions from burning.
2. Preheat the grill to high heat.
3. While the onions are cooking, mix together the ground beef, 2 teaspoons sea salt, the ground black pepper, and 1½ tablespoons teriyaki sauce in a large mixing bowl until well combined. Form the mixture into 4 patties and set aside.
4. Place the burgers on the grill and cook for about 3½ minutes per side, or until they reach your desired doneness.
5. Remove the burgers from the grill and allow them to rest for 5 minutes.
6. Build the burgers with the bottom bun, then a patty, then 1 pineapple ring, ¼ of the caramelized onions, and 2 tablespoons of teriyaki sauce. Repeat until all four burgers are done, and serve.

Ground Beef Quesadillas

Seasoned ground beef, melty cheese, and a crispy, crunchy tortilla make these the perfect budget-friendly dinner. Dip them in sour cream, guacamole, or your favorite salsa.

Prep time: 10 min | Cook time: 20 min | Total time: 30 min | Serves 6–8

1 pound ground beef	Nonstick cooking spray
1 onion, diced	8 large flour tortillas
1 green bell pepper, diced	2 cups shredded Mexican cheese blend
1 (15-ounce) can black beans, drained and rinsed	Sour cream, optional
1 (1-ounce) packet taco seasoning	Guacamole, optional
1 cup salsa	Salsa, optional

1. In a large skillet, cook ground beef, onion, and green pepper until beef is no longer pink and onion is translucent, about 8 minutes. Drain, then add in beans, taco seasoning, and salsa. Let simmer for about 5 minutes to let the flavors meld together.
2. Warm griddle over medium heat and spray with nonstick cooking spray. Place a tortilla on the griddle, sprinkle on shredded cheese, ½ cup per quesadilla, then add ¼ of the ground beef mixture and place another tortilla on top.
3. Flip halfway through cooking. Cook until cheese is melted, and quesadillas are golden brown and warmed through. Repeat with remaining ingredients. Cut quesadillas into quarters or eighths and serve with sour cream, guacamole, or salsa for dipping, or separately.

Multicooker Ravioli Lasagna Soup

All of the lasagna flavor you love, made in a fraction of the time! The ground beef and cheese-filled ravioli make a winning combination in this hearty comfort soup.

Prep time: 10 min | Cook time: 2 min | Pressurize time: 10 min | Total time: 22 min | Serves 8

---

1 pound ground beef

1 yellow onion, diced

2 cloves garlic, minced

1 zucchini, finely diced

1 green bell pepper, finely diced

1 (28-ounce) can crushed tomatoes

1 (14.5-ounce) can petite diced tomatoes

1 (6-ounce) can tomato paste

1 (10.75-ounce) can condensed tomato soup

1 teaspoon white sugar

1½ teaspoons dried basil

1 teaspoon Italian seasoning

½ tablespoon salt

Ground black pepper, to taste

4 cups beef broth

1 (20-ounce) package frozen mini cheese-filled ravioli

Shredded Parmesan cheese, optional garnish

Fresh basil, optional garnish

1. Turn your multicooker on to SAUTÉ. When it's hot, add the ground beef and sauté for about 5 minutes, crumbling as you cook. Add the onion and garlic to the beef and sauté for another 5 minutes.

2. Add in the zucchini, green bell pepper, tomatoes, tomato paste, tomato soup, sugar, dried basil, Italian seasoning, salt, and pepper. Mix well with the meat and onions.

3. Pour the beef broth over everything. Then pour in the frozen ravioli—but don't stir it in. Pasta tends to stick to the bottom of the pot and will give you a burn notice, which is why you add it last and let it float at the top.

4. Place the lid on top and lock into place. Turn the valve to SEAL. Select manual or pressure cook, and set the time for 2 minutes.

5. When cooking ends, carefully turn the valve to VENT to do a quick release of the pressure. Remove the lid.

6. Stir to mix the ravioli in with the other soup ingredients. Serve each bowl of soup topped with freshly grated Parmesan cheese and fresh basil, if desired.

Oven-Baked Beef Tacos

The easiest way to make tacos for a crowd. They're perfectly crunchy and packed with flavor!

Prep time: 10 min | Cook time: 20 min | Total time: 30 min | Serves 6

1 pound ground beef

1 onion, diced

2 teaspoons minced garlic

1 (15-ounce) can black beans, drained and rinsed

1 (1-ounce) packet taco seasoning

1 cup chunky salsa

12 hard taco shells

1½ cups shredded cheddar cheese

2 tomatoes, diced, optional topping

1 cup lettuce, shredded, optional topping

1 (6-ounce) can sliced olives, optional topping

1 cup sour cream, optional topping

1 cup guacamole, optional topping

1. Preheat oven to 400 degrees F.
2. In a large skillet, brown hamburger along with the chopped onion and garlic. Cook until meat is brown and then drain grease from the pan.
3. Add black beans, taco seasoning, and salsa. Mix well and let cook for a couple of minutes so that the flavors can meld and the mixture can thicken.
4. In a large 9x13 baking dish, line up all the taco shells. Fill each one with a couple of scoops of the beef mixture and pack down into the shell. Repeat until all the shells are filled. Top each taco with shredded cheese.
5. Bake for 8–10 minutes, or until all the cheese is melted.
6. Serve with your favorite taco toppings—tomatoes, lettuce, olives, sour cream, guacamole, hot sauce, or whatever you like.

Chicken Dishes

Air Fryer Buffalo
Chicken Wings 51

Air Fryer Chicken Tenders 52

Bacon Ranch Chicken 55

Baked Creamy
Chicken Taquitos 56

BBQ Chicken and Pineapple
Quesadillas 59

Cashew Chicken Skillet
Stir-Fry 60

Chicken Bacon Alfredo
French Bread Pizza 63

Mexican Street Corn
Chicken Tacos 64

Multicooker Apricot Chicken . . . 67

Multicooker Butter Chicken 69

Perfect Air Fryer
Chicken Breasts 70

Tuscan Pasta 73

White Cheddar
Corn Chowder 74

Air Fryer Buffalo Chicken Wings

When you're craving classic, spicy wings, let this be your go-to recipe! Make them quickly—with less mess!—in the air fryer.

Prep time: 10 min | Cook time: 24 min | Total time: 34 min | Serves 4

20 chicken wings

Nonstick cooking spray

¾ cup flour

½ teaspoon cayenne pepper

½ teaspoon garlic powder

½ teaspoon salt

½ cup butter, melted

½ cup red hot sauce, such as Frank's RedHot, plus more for basting, if desired

1. Pat chicken pieces dry with a paper towel. Spray the air fryer insert with nonstick cooking spray.
2. Place the flour, cayenne pepper, garlic powder, and salt into a large (gallon) ziptop bag, seal, and shake to mix. Make sure your chicken wings are completely dry to keep them from getting soggy and add the chicken wings to the bag. Seal the bag and toss until wings are well coated with the flour mixture.
3. Whisk together the melted butter and hot sauce in a small bowl. Dip the wings into the butter–hot sauce mixture and place in the bottom of the air fryer.
4. Set air fryer to 400 degrees F. (preheat for a few minutes if needed) and set timer for 12 minutes.
5. After 12 minutes, use tongs to flip wings over and baste with additional hot sauce for extra flavor.
6. Set air fryer timer for 12 more minutes.
7. Carefully remove chicken wings from air fryer and enjoy! We love to dip these in ranch dressing, but they are great as is.

Air Fryer Chicken Tenders

All the delicious crispiness you want from chicken tenders without the messy oil.

Prep time: 10 min | Cook time: 12 min | Total time: 22 min | Serves 4

---

12 chicken tenders, about 1¼ pounds

Salt and pepper, to taste

2 large eggs, beaten

1 tablespoon water

1 cup Italian breadcrumbs

½ cup grated Parmesan cheese

½ teaspoon salt

¼ teaspoon garlic powder

¼ teaspoon onion powder

1. Season chicken tenders with salt and pepper.
2. In a small bowl, mix together eggs and water.
3. In another medium bowl, mix together breadcrumbs, Parmesan cheese, salt, garlic powder, and onion powder.
4. Dip each chicken tender into the egg mixture, then into the breadcrumb mixture, making sure to shake off any excess breadcrumbs.
5. Place a couple of chicken tenders in the air fryer basket. Put the basket into the inner pot and place the air fryer lid on top. Set the temperature to 400 degrees F. for 6 minutes. Take off the lid, flip each tender over, and cook for another 6 minutes, or until the chicken is cooked through and is golden on the outside.

Note: Depending on the size of your air fryer, you may need to repeat step 5 until all the tenders are cooked.

Bacon Ranch Chicken

Juicy chicken breasts loaded with crispy bacon, ranch seasoning, and melty cheese. This is one chicken recipe you'll come back to again and again.

Prep time: 10 min | Cook time: 20 min | Total time: 30 min | Serves 6

Nonstick cooking spray

1½ pounds boneless, skinless chicken breasts

Salt and pepper, to taste

Onion powder, optional

Garlic powder, optional

¾ cup cream cheese, softened

¾ cup shredded cheddar cheese, divided

5 slices thick cut bacon, cooked and crumbled, divided

1 (1-ounce) packet dry ranch dressing mix

4 green onions, thinly sliced

1. Preheat oven to 400 degrees F.
2. Spray bottom of 9×13 baking pan with nonstick cooking spray.
3. Pound chicken breasts until they are about ¼-inch thick. You want them to all be the same thickness so that they finish cooking at the same time.
4. Place chicken in a single layer in the baking pan and season with salt and pepper. As an option, you can season the chicken with a little bit of onion powder and garlic powder as well.
5. In a medium bowl, mix together the cream cheese, half the shredded cheddar cheese, half the bacon crumbles, and the dry ranch dressing mix.
6. Spread the cream cheese mixture evenly over all the chicken breasts in the pan.
7. Top the chicken with the remaining shredded cheddar cheese.
8. Bake for 20–25 minutes or until chicken is fully cooked to an internal temperature of 165 degrees F.
9. Remove chicken from oven and top with remaining bacon crumbles and green onion.

Baked Creamy Chicken Taquitos

These taquitos are baked, not fried, and they're picky-eater approved. We love them dipped in a creamy cilantro dressing.

Prep time: 10 min | Cook time: 20 min | Total time: 30 min | Serves 6

Nonstick cooking spray

½ package (4 ounces) cream cheese

⅓ cup green salsa

1 tablespoon lime juice

½ teaspoon cumin

1 teaspoon chili powder

½ teaspoon onion powder

¼ teaspoon garlic powder

1 teaspoon dried cilantro

2 green onions, sliced

3 boneless chicken breasts, cooked and shredded

1 cup shredded pepper jack cheese

20 (6-inch) flour tortillas

Salt, to taste

1. Heat oven to 425 degrees F.
2. Line a half-sheet baking pan with foil and lightly coat with nonstick cooking spray.
3. Soften cream cheese in the microwave for about 20–30 seconds so that it's easy to stir.
4. Add green salsa, lime juice, cumin, chili powder, onion powder, and garlic powder. Stir to combine.
5. Add cilantro and green onions.
6. Add chicken and pepper jack cheese and combine well.
7. Place 2–3 tablespoons of chicken mixture on the lower third of a tortilla, keeping it about ½ inch from the edges and roll it up as tight as you can. Place seam side down on the baking sheet.
8. Lay all of the filled taquitos on the baking sheet and make sure they're not touching each other. Spray the tops lightly with cooking spray and sprinkle some salt on top.
9. Place pan in oven and bake for 15–20 minutes or until crisp and the ends begin to turn golden brown.

BBQ Chicken and Pineapple Quesadillas

Grilled barbecue chicken, fresh slices of pineapple, and melty cheese in a warm tortilla make this quick meal a family favorite. We love adding some jalapeño pepper for a little kick, too.

Prep time: 10 min | Cook time: 20 min | Total time: 30 min | Serves 6

1 pineapple, sliced

3 boneless, skinless chicken breasts

Salt and pepper, to taste

1 cup barbecue sauce, such as Sweet Baby Ray's

Nonstick cooking spray

12 (8-inch) flour tortillas

3 cups shredded Monterey Jack cheese

¼ cup sliced jalapeño peppers

1. Grill your pineapple by cutting it into slices, sticking it on skewers, and grilling over low heat. Cut into smaller, bite-size pieces and set aside.
2. Season chicken breasts with salt and pepper and place on a grill or pan on medium heat. Brush with barbecue sauce and grill or cook on one side, then brush other side and grill or cook on opposite side until done. Remove from heat and cut into thin strips or small pieces and set aside.
3. Warm a griddle to medium heat and spray with nonstick cooking spray. Place tortillas on griddle, sprinkle on ½ cup shredded cheese per quesadilla, and add chicken, pineapple, and jalapeño slices.
4. Add a small drizzle of barbecue sauce and place another tortilla on top. Flip halfway through cooking. Cook until cheese is melted and quesadillas are golden brown and warmed through.

Cashew Chicken Skillet Stir-Fry

This stir-fry recipe has a delicious soy sauce and peanut butter taste, and it's a great way to get a delicious serving of veggies.

Prep time: 15 min | Cook time: 15 min | Total time: 30 min | Serves 6

STIR-FRY

1½ tablespoons olive oil

1½ pounds boneless, skinless chicken breasts,
   cut into bite-size pieces

Salt and pepper, to taste

½ cup cashew pieces,
   preferably unsalted or lightly salted

4 garlic cloves, minced

3 cups broccoli florets

1 red bell pepper, thinly sliced

1 yellow bell pepper, thinly sliced

1 cup sugar snap peas

1 cup shredded carrots

5 green onions, sliced

SAUCE

6 tablespoons less sodium soy sauce

¼ cup natural peanut butter

3 tablespoons honey

1½ teaspoons sesame oil

¼ teaspoon ground ginger

3 tablespoons water

1. Place a large skillet on the stove top and heat to medium-high. Add olive oil.
2. Season the chicken with salt and pepper, then add the chicken and cashews to the skillet. We like to add the cashews at the same time as the chicken, but you can add them with the vegetables if you prefer.
3. Cook for 4–5 minutes, stirring occasionally, then add the garlic and cook for about 30 seconds more. The chicken will not be fully cooked yet, but that's okay.
4. Add in all the vegetables and sauté for 5–7 minutes, or until all the vegetables are tender and the chicken is fully cooked to an internal temperature of 165 degrees F.
5. In a medium bowl, mix together all the ingredients for the homemade sauce, then drizzle over the chicken and vegetables.
6. Continue to stir in the skillet until everything is heated through.

Chicken Bacon Alfredo French Bread Pizza

Crusty French bread topped with creamy Alfredo sauce makes this pizza a win in our book!

Prep time: 10 min | Cook time: 10 min | Total time: 20 min | Serves 6

---

1 loaf French bread

1 (15-ounce) jar Alfredo sauce

1 teaspoon garlic salt

1 teaspoon Italian seasoning

4 cups shredded mozzarella cheese

2 cups shredded rotisserie (or any cooked) chicken

2 Roma tomatoes, diced

5 green onions, thinly sliced

1 (3-ounce) jar bacon bits (about ⅓ cup)

½ cup grated Parmesan cheese

1. Preheat oven to 400 degrees F.
2. Cut loaf of French bread lengthwise and place on a half-sheet baking pan, cut sides up. Spread Alfredo sauce evenly over bread (as much or as little as you like). Sprinkle garlic salt and Italian seasoning over sauce.
3. Top with mozzarella cheese, cooked chicken, tomatoes, green onions, bacon bits, and Parmesan cheese.
4. Cook for about 10 minutes or until cheese starts to melt.
5. Cut into slices and serve.

Mexican Street Corn Chicken Tacos

Flavorful chicken topped with the perfect Mexican street corn makes these chicken tacos unforgettable.

Prep time: 15 min | Cook time: 15 min | Total time: 30 min | Serves 6

CHICKEN

1 tablespoon olive oil

3 boneless, skinless chicken breasts, about 1½ pounds, cooked and shredded, or sliced

1 teaspoon cumin

1½ teaspoons chili powder

1 teaspoon garlic powder

½ teaspoon salt

½ teaspoon pepper

MEXICAN STREET CORN

2 tablespoons olive oil

1 (16-ounce) package frozen corn

3 tablespoons mayonnaise

4 ounces crumbled cotija cheese (could also use feta cheese)

2 tablespoons lime juice—fresh is best

1 tablespoon finely chopped jalapeño pepper

⅓ cup finely chopped fresh cilantro

2 tablespoons finely chopped red onion

2 garlic cloves, minced

½ teaspoon chili powder

Salt and pepper, to taste

TACOS

6 (8-inch) corn or flour tortillas

2 avocados, sliced

Cotija cheese, optional topping

Fresh cilantro, optional topping

1. In a skillet over medium heat, heat oil. Add shredded, cooked chicken, cumin, chili powder, garlic powder, salt, and pepper. Stir and cook until completely heated through and all the chicken is coated in seasonings. Remove from heat, cover with aluminum foil to keep warm, and set aside while you prepare the corn.

2. To make the street corn, in a skillet over medium heat, heat oil.

3. Add frozen corn and cook until corn starts to char, stirring occasionally (about 7–8 minutes).

4. While the corn is cooking, mix together mayonnaise, cheese, lime juice, jalapeño, cilantro, red onion, garlic, chili powder, salt, and pepper in a large bowl. When corn is done, gently fold it in with other ingredients.

5. Lay tortilla out on a plate. Top with ¼ cup chicken, about 3 tablespoons Mexican street corn, sliced avocados, cotija cheese, and fresh cilantro.

Multicooker Apricot Chicken

This dump-and-go recipe is only 5 ingredients and sweetly simple. It's sure to become a staple at your house.

Prep time: 5 min | Cook time: 10 min | Pressurize time: 10 min | Total time: 25 min | Serves 6

1½ cups apricot preserves

1 cup Russian or French dressing

1 (1-ounce) packet onion soup mix

1½ pounds boneless, skinless chicken breasts

½ cup chicken broth

1. In a medium-size bowl, mix together the apricot preserves, Russian dressing, and dry onion soup mix packet.
2. Place the chicken breasts in a multicooker and add ½ cup chicken broth.
3. Pour the apricot preserve mixture over the chicken.
4. Lock the lid in place and turn the pressure valve to SEAL. Set to cook for 10 minutes. When the timer sounds, allow the pressure to release naturally for 5 minutes and then turn the pressure valve to VENT to let the remaining steam out of the multicooker.
5. Shred the chicken and stir until it's combined with the apricot mixture, then serve over rice.

Multicooker Butter Chicken

Get rich, creamy butter chicken without spending hours in the kitchen—let your multicooker do most of the work! The spiced sauce will bring the flavors of your favorite takeout right to your table in no time.

Prep time: 5 min | Cook time: 20 min | Natural release: 5 min | Total time: 30 min | Serves 6

4 tablespoons butter

1 onion, diced

5 cloves garlic, minced

2 pounds chicken thighs or chicken breasts, cut into bite-size pieces

1 (15-ounce) can tomato sauce

3 tablespoons tomato paste

2 tablespoons red curry paste

2 teaspoons garam masala

1½ teaspoons ground ginger

1 teaspoon salt

½ teaspoon smoked paprika

½ cup heavy cream

Fresh cilantro, optional garnish

1. Set your multicooker to SAUTÉ and add butter, onion, and garlic. Sauté for approximately 5 minutes until the onions are tender. Press OFF to cancel the sauté.

2. Add the chicken, tomato sauce, tomato paste, red curry paste, garam masala, ground ginger, salt, and smoked paprika to the pot. Lock the lid in place and turn the pressure valve to SEAL. Cook for 7 minutes.

3. When the timer sounds, release the pressure naturally for 5 minutes and then turn the valve on top to VENT to let the remaining steam out of the multicooker.

4. Remove the lid and use a slotted spoon to remove the chicken from the sauce and set aside.

5. Add the heavy cream to the pot and use an immersion blender to puree the sauce until smooth.

6. Set the multicooker to SAUTÉ and stir the sauce while simmering for 7–10 minutes or until it thickens. Press OFF to cancel the sauté.

7. Add the chicken back to the sauce, stir together, and serve with a garnish of cilantro, if desired.

Note: If you do not have an immersion blender, pour the contents of the inner pot into a blender, and then pour it back into the inner pot once it's smooth. Be careful to only fill the blender about halfway (work in batches if needed) to avoid splatters.

Perfect Air Fryer Chicken Breasts

This super simple chicken breast is seasoned to perfection and comes out tender and juicy every time.

Prep time: 5 min | Cook time: 15 min | Total time: 20 min | Serves 2–4

---

2 boneless, skinless medium-size chicken breasts

1½ tablespoons olive oil

2 teaspoons salt

1 teaspoon ground black pepper

2 teaspoons garlic powder

2 teaspoons oregano

1. Preheat your air fryer to 375 degrees F.
2. While the air fryer is preheating, add the chicken, olive oil, salt, pepper, garlic powder, and oregano to a mixing bowl. Toss it all together until the chicken is thoroughly coated in olive oil and seasoning.
3. Place the chicken in the air fryer and cook at 375 degrees F. for 7 minutes.
4. Flip the chicken and cook for an additional 7 minutes.
5. Check the temperature of the chicken by sticking a meat thermometer into the thickest part of the largest breast. If the temperature reads 165 degrees F., the chicken is done. If it's not there yet, refer to the next step.
6. If the chicken has not yet reached an internal temperature of 165 degrees F., air fry it for another 2 minutes and check the temperature again. Repeat if necessary until the chicken is cooked through.

Tuscan Pasta

Creamy, cheesy garlic sauce, sun-dried tomatoes, and grilled chicken make this pasta an instant favorite. The best part is that it can double as a freezer meal!

Prep time: 10 min | Cook time: 20 min | Total time: 30 min | Serves 8

1 (16-ounce) package farfalle (bow tie) pasta

4 tablespoons butter

4 garlic cloves, finely minced

1½ teaspoons dried basil

1 (8-ounce) package cream cheese, softened and cut into small cubes

1 (8-ounce) jar sun-dried tomatoes, drained, rinsed, and chopped

2 cups milk

8 ounces Parmesan cheese, grated

½ teaspoon ground black pepper

½ teaspoon salt, more if needed, to taste

1 cup cooked and cubed chicken

1. Cook pasta according to package directions. While it's cooking, prepare the sauce.
2. In a medium pot or skillet, melt butter over medium heat. Add garlic and cook for about 2 minutes, stirring the whole time. Stir in dried basil. Add cream cheese, stirring with a whisk until the mixture is smooth. It will look curdled at first, but with constant whisking for 2–3 minutes, it will become a smooth, creamy paste. Stir in sun-dried tomatoes.
3. Keep cooking over medium heat and add milk, whisking quickly and constantly until blended into the sauce. Stir in the Parmesan cheese, pepper, and salt. Cook over medium heat, stirring until the cheese is melted and the sauce is the desired consistency, 5–10 minutes.
4. Serve over the hot, cooked pasta. Sprinkle cooked, cubed chicken over top.

White Cheddar Corn Chowder

With a Tex-Mex blend of green chiles, fire-roasted tomatoes, creamed corn, and tortilla chips, this soup will warm you up on even the coldest of days.

Prep time: 10 min | Cook time: 20 min | Total time: 30 min | Serves 8

1 tablespoon butter

½ onion, chopped

2 teaspoons minced garlic

1 cup chicken broth

1 teaspoon ground cumin

2 boneless, skinless chicken breasts, cooked and cubed

2 cups half-and-half

2 cups shredded white sharp cheddar cheese

1 (14.75-ounce) can cream style corn, undrained

1 (4-ounce) can chopped green chiles, undrained

1 (14.5-ounce) can fire-roasted tomatoes, drained

1 tablespoon chopped cilantro

2 cups tortilla chips (or strips)

1. In a large saucepot, melt butter over medium heat. Add onions and sauté until soft. Add garlic and sauté for another minute.
2. Add chicken broth and cumin, then bring to a boil. Reduce heat and cover, simmering for about 5 minutes.
3. Stir in the chicken, half-and-half, cheese, corn, chiles, and tomatoes. Cook and stir over medium-low heat until the cheese is melted.
4. Serve warm in bowls garnished with cilantro and tortilla chips or strips.

Meatless Dishes

Crispy Bean and
Cheese Burritos 79

Fettucine Alfredo 80

Fresh Cajun Pasta 83

Seven-Layer Dip Burritos 84

Sheet-Pan Pancakes 87

Spinach and Tomato
Tortellini 88

White Cheddar Shells
and Cheese 90

Crispy Bean and Cheese Burritos

These delicious burritos are filled with rice, beans, avocado, and cheese, then pan-fried until they're perfectly golden, warm, and crispy.

Prep time: 10 min | Cook time: 14 min | Total time: 24 min | Serves 6

1 (3.5-ounce) boil-in-bag brown rice, such as Success

1 cup salsa

⅓ cup chopped cilantro

1 avocado, diced

1 tablespoon fresh lime juice

6 (10-inch) soft flour tortillas

2 cups shredded Mexican blend cheese

1 (15-ounce) can black beans, drained and rinsed

Nonstick cooking spray

1. Cook the boil-in-bag brown rice according to package directions, about 10 minutes.
2. Drain and place in a medium-size bowl, add the salsa and cilantro and mix well, then set aside.
3. Put the diced avocado in a bowl, add the fresh lime juice, and toss well. Set aside.
4. Place the six tortillas on a work surface. Sprinkle ⅓ cup shredded cheese in the center of each tortilla in a 3-inch strip. Top the cheese with ¼ cup black beans.
5. Place a heaping ⅓ cup rice mixture over the beans.
6. Divide the avocado pieces evenly over the six tortillas.
7. Fold up opposite sides of tortilla and then the bottom and roll up to enclose the filling. Repeat until all burritos are rolled.
8. Coat the top and bottom of the burritos with nonstick cooking spray. Place 3 burritos in the skillet, seam side down. Cook for about 1 minute or until lightly browned and crisp. Turn the burritos and cook another minute until golden brown. Repeat with 3 remaining burritos.

Fettuccine Alfredo

You'll never use Alfredo sauce from a can again after you taste this! It's quick, inexpensive—and there are never any leftovers!

Prep time: 5 min | Cook time: 12 min | Total time: 17 min | Serves 6

1½ (16-ounce) packages fettuccine pasta (24 ounces total)

½ cup butter

1½ cups heavy whipping cream

1 teaspoon minced garlic

½ teaspoon Italian seasoning

Salt and pepper, to taste

1½ cups shredded Parmesan cheese

2 ounces cream cheese

Fresh parsley, for garnish

1. Bring a large pot of water to boil. Salt generously, then add fettuccine and cook until al dente according to package directions.
2. In a separate saucepan over low heat, add butter and cream and stir until the butter is melted. Whisk in garlic, Italian seasoning, and salt and pepper.
3. Add in shredded Parmesan cheese and cream cheese, then stir until completely combined.
4. Add the cooked pasta to the sauce and toss until coated, then serve immediately.
5. Garnish with chopped parsley and extra Parmesan cheese, if desired.

Note: We've found that using freshly grated Parmesan gives the best results for a smooth, creamy Alfredo sauce.

Fresh Cajun Pasta

Don't be intimidated by making homemade pasta sauce! With just a few simple ingredients like Roma tomatoes, garlic, and parsley you can whip this up in no time.

Prep time: 15 min | Cook time: 15 min | Total time: 30 min | Serves 4

---

1 (16-ounce) package vermicelli pasta

2 tablespoons olive oil

1 teaspoon minced garlic

10 Roma tomatoes, chopped

Salt, to taste

1 tablespoon chopped parsley

1 tablespoon Cajun seasoning

½ cup grated Parmesan cheese

½ cup grated mozzarella cheese

1. Bring a large pot of water to a boil. Generously salt the water, then add pasta and cook al dente according to package directions.
2. While the pasta is boiling, heat olive oil and garlic in a large saucepan. Once the garlic is fragrant and starting to brown, add the chopped tomatoes.
3. Simmer for about 10 minutes, and then mash tomatoes with a fork.
4. Add salt, parsley, and Cajun seasoning and simmer for about 5 more minutes.
5. Remove from heat and serve over pasta.
6. Top with Parmesan and mozzarella cheese.

Seven-Layer Dip Burritos

If you love seven-layer dip, you're going to love these burritos! Layers of beans, guacamole, tomatoes, cheese, sour cream, lettuce, and olives make this meatless meal a winner.

Prep time: 15 min | Total time: 15 min | Serves 8

---

8 (10-inch) flour tortillas

2 (16-ounce) cans refried beans

1 cup guacamole

2 tomatoes, diced

2 cups shredded cheddar cheese

1 cup light sour cream

1 head iceberg lettuce, shredded

1 (6-ounce) can black olives, drained and sliced

1. Place refried beans in a covered, microwave-safe bowl and heat them in 30-second increments, stirring after each increment, until hot, about 1½ minutes.

2. Spread a layer of beans on a tortilla. Add a layer of guacamole, tomatoes, cheese, sour cream, chopped lettuce, and sliced olives.

3. Fold up opposite sides of the tortilla and then the bottom, then roll up to enclose the filling. Repeat until all burritos are made. Serve immediately.

Sheet-Pan Pancakes

These fluffy sheet-pan pancakes feed a large group without worrying about flipping! We love how versatile they are—everyone can add their favorite toppings to make them their own.

Prep time: 15 min | Cook time: 15 min | Total time: 30 min | Serves 8

Nonstick cooking spray

2 eggs, separated

¼ cup sugar

3½ teaspoons vanilla extract

4 tablespoons salted butter, melted

2 cups buttermilk

2 cups all-purpose flour

2 teaspoons baking powder

1 teaspoon baking soda

½ teaspoon salt

½ teaspoon cinnamon

1. Preheat the oven to 425 degrees F. and line a half-sheet baking pan with aluminum foil. Spray the aluminum foil with nonstick cooking spray.
2. In a small bowl, beat the egg whites on high speed until stiff peaks form. Set aside.
3. In a large bowl, combine and whisk together the egg yolks, sugar, vanilla, and butter until smooth. Slowly mix in the buttermilk.
4. Combine the dry ingredients and whisk together. Then whisk the dry ingredients into the wet ingredients.
5. Gently fold in the whipped egg whites.
6. Pour the batter into the prepared sheet-pan and bake for 15 minutes or until a toothpick inserted in the center comes out clean.
7. Slice into eight equal pieces and serve with butter, maple syrup, and any other favorite pancake toppings.

Spinach and Tomato Tortellini

A cozy, meatless meal that combines cheese-filled tortellini with fresh spinach and juicy tomatoes in a simple, creamy sauce.

Prep time: 10 min | Cook time: 15 min | Total time: 25 min | Serves 6

---

1 (20-ounce) package cheese tortellini

1 teaspoon olive oil

1 (14.5-ounce) can diced tomatoes, drained

2–3 cups chopped baby spinach

2 teaspoons minced garlic

2 teaspoons Italian seasoning

Salt and pepper, to taste

1½ cups half-and-half

¼ cup grated Parmesan cheese

2 tablespoons flour

1. Cook tortellini according to package directions.
2. While the tortellini cooks, heat the olive oil over medium heat in a large saucepan. Add the diced tomatoes, spinach, garlic, Italian seasoning, salt, and pepper. Cook and stir until the garlic is fragrant and the spinach is wilted.
3. Stir in the half-and-half and Parmesan cheese. Whisk in the flour to help thicken the mixture.
4. Drain the tortellini and add it to the spinach mixture. Stir until tortellini is coated and mixture is heated through. Serve warm.

White Cheddar Shells and Cheese

The ultimate kid-approved dinner the whole family will enjoy. The star of this recipe is the from-scratch white cheddar sauce.

Prep time: 10 min | Cook time: 20 min | Total time: 30 min | Serves 8

1 (16-ounce) package shell pasta

½ cup butter

6 tablespoons flour

4½ cups milk

2½ cups shredded white cheddar cheese

1½ cups shredded Parmesan cheese

1 teaspoon ground mustard

1 teaspoon salt

1 pinch pepper

1. Cook pasta according to package instructions. Drain and set aside.
2. Make a roux by heating ½ cup butter in a saucepan until melted. Slowly whisk in the flour until blended and bubbly. Whisk constantly until roux is a light brown, and then slowly add in the milk, whisking out any lumps. Add in cheeses, mustard, salt, and pepper and whisk until smooth.
3. Add cooked pasta to the sauce and stir until completely combined.
4. Serve topped with extra Parmesan cheese and a sprinkle of pepper.

Pork Dishes

Air Fryer Pizzas 95

Baked Ham and Cheese
   Croissant Sandwiches 96

Braided Pizza Loaf 99

Easy Sausage Tortellini Soup . . . 101

Garlic Lime Pork Chops 102

Grilled Honey Mustard
   Pork Chops 105

Hot Italian Trio Sandwiches 107

Multicooker Loaded
   Mac and Cheese 108

Pineapple Pasta Skillet 111

Pizza Skillet Pasta 112

Szechuan Pork and Noodles . . . 115

Tuscan White Bean Soup 116

Air Fryer Pizzas

Perfect for a quick dinner or a fun family night, simple pizzas can be customized easily, so everyone in your family is happy.

Prep time: 10 min | Cook time: 14 min | Total time: 24 min | Serves 4

1 (16.30-ounce) can premade biscuit dough, such as Pillsbury Flaky Grands

Nonstick cooking spray

1 cup pizza sauce, such as Ragu or Contadina

2 cups shredded mozzarella cheese

1 (5-ounce) package sliced pepperoni

1 cup freshly grated Parmesan cheese

1. Open the package of biscuits and separate the biscuits. Roll each into an approximately 4-inch circle.
2. Preheat the air fryer to 410 degrees F. and spray the basket liberally with nonstick cooking spray.
3. While the air fryer is preheating, top each biscuit round with 2 tablespoons pizza sauce, ¼ cup mozzarella, 4–5 pieces of pepperoni, and a sprinkle of Parmesan.
4. Arrange 4 pizzas in the basket of your air fryer (2 if it is a smaller machine) and fry for 7 minutes or until the biscuit dough has become firm enough to pick up without falling apart and the cheese has gotten nice and melty. Repeat with the remaining pizzas.

Note: Serving size is two small pizzas.

Baked Ham and Cheese Croissant Sandwiches

You can throw these sandwiches together in a matter of minutes, and with just a few simple ingredients, you've got an elevated sandwich that's great for breakfast, brunch, or dinner.

Prep time: 5 min | Cook time: 15 min | Total time: 20 min | Serves 6

6 large croissants

4 ounces cream cheese, softened

1 tablespoon Dijon mustard, depending on how much mustard flavor you prefer

½ pound thinly sliced ham

6 slices cheddar cheese or Swiss cheese

1. Heat oven to 350 degrees F.
2. Cover a half-sheet baking pan with aluminum foil.
3. Split your croissants in half and place on the baking sheet, cut sides up.
4. In a small bowl, mix together cream cheese and Dijon mustard. Spread some of the cream cheese mixture on one half of each croissant.
5. Layer sliced ham and sliced cheese on top of cream cheese mixture.
6. Top with the other half of the croissant.
7. Bake for 12–15 minutes and serve immediately.

Braided Pizza Loaf

This fun take on pizza is made even easier with premade refrigerated dough, then topped with layers of sauce, toppings, and gooey mozzarella cheese.

Prep time: 10 min | Cook time: 20 min | Total time: 30 min | Serves 6

1 (13.8-ounce) package refrigerated pizza dough, such as Pillsbury Classic Pizza Crust

Nonstick cooking spray

½ cup pizza sauce, such as Ragu or Contadina

1½ cups shredded mozzarella cheese

3 ounces sliced pepperoni

1 tablespoon olive oil

½ teaspoon garlic powder

1 teaspoon Italian seasoning

2 tablespoons grated Parmesan cheese

1. Preheat oven to 400 degrees F. Spray a half-sheet baking pan with nonstick cooking spray.
2. Unroll pizza dough on the half-sheet pan.
3. Spread pizza sauce down the middle third of your dough lengthwise, leaving an approximately 2-inch space on either side of the dough.
4. Add mozzarella cheese and pepperoni on top of sauce.
5. Using a pizza cutter, cut 1-inch wide diagonal strips up each side of the uncovered dough.
6. Alternating sides, fold the strips up and over sauce and toppings to get a braided look.
7. Brush the top of the braided dough with olive oil and sprinkle with the garlic powder, Italian seasoning, and Parmesan cheese
8. Bake for 15–20 minutes or until golden brown.
9. Let cool for a few minutes, then cut into slices and serve.

Easy Sausage Tortellini Soup

Packed full of veggies, and with cheesy tortellini and a delicious, creamy tomato base, this soup is a favorite with kids and adults.

Prep time: 5 min | Cook time: 25 min | Total time: 30 min | Serves 8

1 (1-pound) package ground pork sausage

1 tablespoon butter

1 yellow onion, finely diced

1 cup shredded carrots

2 celery ribs, finely diced

3 garlic cloves, finely minced

1 tablespoon Italian seasoning

¼ cup flour

4 cups chicken broth

1 (14-ounce) can diced tomatoes

1 (6-ounce) can tomato paste

1 cup heavy cream (or half-and-half, but the soup will not be as thick and creamy)

1 (9-ounce) package three cheese tortellini

2–3 cups roughly chopped baby spinach

Salt and pepper, to taste

Freshly grated Parmesan cheese, optional topping

1. In a large stockpot, cook the sausage over medium heat until sausage is no longer pink. Drain, if desired, and remove sausage from pot. Set aside.
2. Add butter to pot and let melt over medium heat. Add in onion, carrots, and celery. Sauté until tender.
3. Add in garlic and Italian seasoning, cook for about 1 minute more.
4. Sprinkle in flour with the vegetables and mix until all vegetables are lightly coated.
5. Pour in chicken broth, then add in tomatoes and tomato paste and stir.
6. Add in heavy cream, tortellini, and spinach and bring to a simmer for about 6–7 minutes, or until tortellini is cooked and spinach is wilted. Stir in sausage.
7. Season with salt and pepper before serving.
8. As a tasty option, top each bowl with freshly grated Parmesan cheese.

Garlic Lime Pork Chops

These pork chops have a delicious tangy flavor and a hint of savory goodness. This simple yet flavorful dish is inexpensive and makes a great weeknight meal.

Prep time: 10 min | Cook time: 10 min | Total time: 20 min | Serves 4

4 (6-ounce) lean, boneless pork chops

4 garlic cloves, crushed

1 teaspoon cumin

1 teaspoon chili powder

1 teaspoon paprika

Salt and pepper, to taste

1 lime, juiced

Zest of 1 lime

1. Trim any fat from pork.
2. In a large bowl combine garlic, cumin, chili powder, paprika, salt, and pepper. Then add in the squeezed lime juice and zest.
3. Let pork chops marinate in this mixture for at least 20 minutes.
4. Line broiler pan with foil for easy cleanup.
5. Place pork chops on the broiler pan and broil about 4–5 minutes on each side or until nicely browned.

Note: This recipe is written for broiled pork chops, however, they can also be grilled for the same amount of time.

Grilled Honey Mustard Pork Chops

These basted pork chops are covered in a sweet, tangy sauce that caramelizes perfectly on the grill.

Prep time: 10 min | Cook time: 12 min | Total time: 22 min | Serves 4

4 (6-ounce) lean, boneless pork chops

Salt and pepper, to taste

1 tablespoon liquid smoke

3 tablespoons Dijon mustard

1½ tablespoons honey

2 teaspoons minced garlic

1. Sprinkle pork chops generously with salt and pepper, then give them a good dousing of liquid smoke and set aside.
2. Heat oven broiler to high or preheat grill. Combine mustard, honey, and garlic together in a small bowl and set aside.
3. Place pork chops on a broiler pan/grill and cook for 4–5 minutes. Turn over and cook for another 4–5 minutes. The internal temperature should be at least 165 degrees F. (barely pink inside). Do not over-cook, or they will become tough and dry.
4. Baste chops with the honey mustard mixture and cook an additional minute on each side.
5. Remove from heat and allow to rest a few minutes to seal in the juices.

Hot Italian Trio Sandwiches

These deli-style sandwiches are packed with layers of savory meats, cheese, and peppers and toasted to perfection. Try substituting different meats for different flavors in this one!

Prep time: 10 min | Cook time: 22 min | Total time: 32 min | Serves 4

½ cup salted butter, melted

1 tablespoon Italian seasoning

½ teaspoon ground black pepper

4 hoagie rolls

12 slices soppressata

12 slices salami

12 slices prosciutto

12 slices fresh mozzarella

½ cup freshly grated Parmesan cheese

8 leaves romaine lettuce, shredded

2 Roma tomatoes, sliced

½ cup sliced mild pepperoncini

1. Preheat oven to 350 degrees F. Line a half-sheet baking pan with aluminum foil.
2. Whisk together the butter, Italian seasoning, and pepper.
3. Open the hoagie rolls and place them cut sides up on the prepared baking sheet. Brush the butter mixture over both sides of each roll. Bake for 7 minutes or until golden brown.
4. Remove the rolls from the oven and arrange 3 slices of soppressata, 3 slices of salami, and 3 slices of prosciutto inside each roll. Top the meat with 3 slices of mozzarella per sandwich and a sprinkle of Parmesan.
5. Gently close the rolls, wrap each sandwich in foil, and bake for 15 minutes or until the cheese has melted.
6. Gently unwrap the foil, open the sandwiches, and top with lettuce, tomato slices, and pepperoncini. Close the sandwiches and serve.

Multicooker Loaded Mac and Cheese

Creamy, cheesy, bacon-y goodness, all made in the multicooker—what's not to love?

Prep time: 10 min | Cook time: 10 min | Pressurize time: 10 min | Total time: 30 min | Serves 6

MAC AND CHEESE

2½ cups (about 8 ounces) elbow macaroni

3 cups chicken broth

½ teaspoon onion powder

1 teaspoon dry mustard

¼ teaspoon seasoning salt

¼ teaspoon pepper

4 ounces cream cheese

1 tablespoon butter

½ cup milk

3 cups shredded cheddar cheese

CRUMB TOPPING

2 tablespoons butter

½ cup panko breadcrumbs

OTHER TOPPINGS

¼ cup minced chives

6 slices bacon, cooked and crumbled

1. Add uncooked macaroni, chicken broth, onion powder, dry mustard, seasoning salt, and pepper to the multicooker.
2. Cover, set to SEAL, and cook on high pressure for 5 minutes.
3. Once cooking time is completed, set pressure valve to VENT to quick release the pressure.
4. Add cream cheese and butter to the macaroni and remaining water. Mix until combined.
5. Stir in milk and shredded cheese until cheese is melted and everything is well combined.
6. For crumb topping, add butter and breadcrumbs to a pan over medium-high heat and cook for 2–3 minutes or until breadcrumbs are golden brown, stirring constantly. Remove crumbs from heat.
7. Divide macaroni and cheese into equal portions in bowls or on plates and sprinkle crumb mixture on top.
8. Sprinkle chives and bacon crumbles on top and serve.

Pineapple Pasta Skillet

This pineapple pasta skillet is a delightful mix of sweet and savory, with tender ham, juicy pineapple, and a creamy sauce that ties it all together. It's an easy, one-pan meal that's packed with flavor.

Prep time: 15 min | **Cook time:** 15 min | **Total time:** 30 min | **Serves 6**

1 tablespoon olive oil

2 cups cubed, cooked ham

1 (8-ounce) can tomato sauce

2 cups chicken broth

½ teaspoon onion powder

½ teaspoon garlic salt

¼ teaspoon pepper

1 (16-ounce) package rigatoni pasta

1 (20-ounce) can pineapple chunks, drained

1 cup shredded mozzarella cheese

2 tablespoons chopped cilantro leaves, for garnish

1. Heat stove to medium-high.
2. In a large skillet or saucepan, add olive oil and cubed ham and cook until the ham starts to brown.
3. Add the tomato sauce, chicken broth, onion powder, garlic salt, and pepper, and mix until well combined.
4. Add the pasta to the mixture and continue stirring until all the ingredients are mixed.
5. Bring the mixture to a boil and cover with a lid.
6. Boil, covered, for about 15 minutes or until the pasta is soft.
7. Remove lid and stir in pineapple.
8. Remove the skillet from the heat and top with mozzarella cheese and stir until it melts into the pasta.
9. Before serving, sprinkle with cilantro as a garnish.

Pizza Skillet Pasta

All your favorite pizza flavors served as a hearty pasta dish. Add or subtract favorite toppings to make it your own.

Prep time: 10 min | Cook time: 20 min | Total time: 30 min | Serves 6

1 (1-pound) package ground Italian sausage

1 onion, diced

1 green bell pepper, diced

2 teaspoons minced garlic

8 ounces sliced fresh mushrooms

1¼ cups uncooked elbow macaroni

1 (24-ounce) jar marinara sauce, such as Prego or Barilla

1¾ cups water

1 (2.25-ounce) can sliced black olives, such as Pearls, drained

1 cup shredded mozzarella cheese

1 cup shredded cheddar cheese

20 slices pepperoni

½ cup grated Parmesan cheese

1. Heat oven to 400 degrees F.
2. In a large ovenproof skillet, brown sausage, onion, bell pepper, garlic, and sliced mushrooms over medium-high heat for about 5 minutes or until meat is cooked through. Drain excess fat.
3. Add in macaroni, marinara sauce, water, and olives and cook for about 10 minutes or until macaroni is soft.
4. Top with shredded cheeses, pepperoni, and Parmesan cheese.
5. Bake in oven for about 15 minutes until cheese is melted and bubbly. Serve hot.

Szechuan Pork and Noodles

A delicious, spicy twist to stir-fry—full of veggies and packed with amazing Asian-inspired flavor.

Prep time: 10 min | Cook time: 21 min | Total time: 31 min | Serves 6

---

1 (16-ounce) package linguine pasta

2 tablespoons butter

4 boneless pork chops, cut into bite-size pieces

2 tablespoons olive oil

1 yellow onion, diced

2 green bell peppers, diced

1¾ cups teriyaki sauce, such as Kikkoman or San-J

2 teaspoons minced garlic

1 teaspoon paprika

2 cups steamed broccoli florets

1. Cook the linguine noodles according to the directions on the package.
2. While the noodles are cooking, melt butter in a large skillet over medium-high heat. Add the pork and cook until it is white and no longer pink on the inside, about 5–8 minutes.
3. Remove the pork from the skillet and set aside.
4. Add olive oil to the same skillet over medium heat.
5. Add the onion and bell pepper and sauté until soft, about 8 minutes.
6. Once the vegetables are done, add the cooked pork back to the skillet.
7. Add in the teriyaki sauce, minced garlic, and paprika. Stir well. Reduce heat to medium-low and continue to cook for 5–8 more minutes, or until marinade is thoroughly heated and slightly thickened.
8. Fold in steamed broccoli.
9. When linguine is done cooking, drain the water and add noodles into the pork-sauce mixture.
10. Stir to combine and serve.

Tuscan White Bean Soup

Packed with flavor from the tender white beans, fresh garlic, and sausage. Even though this is an easy soup recipe, it makes a great hearty dinner.

Prep time: 5 mins | Cook time: 30 mins | Total time: 35 mins | Serves: 8

---

3 tablespoons olive oil, divided

1 pound Italian sausage

1 yellow onion, diced

3 medium carrots, sliced into rounds

3 ribs celery, sliced

2 cloves garlic, minced

1 teaspoon salt

½ teaspoon pepper

1 tablespoon Italian seasoning

2 heaping handfuls chopped Tuscan kale

8 cups chicken stock

2 (15-ounce cans) cannellini beans, drained and rinsed

Salt and pepper, to taste

1. Heat 1½ tablespoons olive oil over medium-high heat in a large, heavy-bottomed soup pot or Dutch oven. Add the sausage and sauté until cooked through and nicely caramelized, breaking it apart with a wooden spoon as you go. Use a slotted spoon to transfer the cooked sausage to a bowl. Set aside.
2. Add the remaining olive oil to the pot, followed by the onion, carrot, celery, and garlic. Season with salt, pepper, and Italian seasoning. Sauté until the veggies have softened. Add the kale and sauté until it has wilted substantially. If the veggies start to burn, add a splash of chicken stock.
3. Stir in the chicken stock, cannellini beans, and cooked Italian sausage.
4. Bring the soup to a boil and then reduce the heat to low. Simmer for 15 minutes.
5. Taste the soup and season with salt and pepper to taste.

Seafood Dishes

Air Fryer Coconut Shrimp......121

Baked Salmon................ 122

Lemon Garlic Shrimp Pasta 125

Multicooker Salmon Bowls 126

New England Clam Chowder... 128

Pan-Seared Mahi-Mahi 131

Parmesan Fish Sticks
  with Tartar Sauce 132

Sheet-Pan Shrimp Fajitas 135

Air Fryer Coconut Shrimp

Coated in sweet coconut flakes, this shrimp is light, crunchy, and perfect for dipping in your favorite sauce.

Prep time: 10 min | Cook time: 10 min | Total time: 20 min | Serves 4

½ cup all-purpose flour

1 teaspoon salt

¼ teaspoon ground black pepper

1 cup unsweetened shredded coconut

¾ cup panko breadcrumbs

2 eggs

1 tablespoon water

1 pound uncooked jumbo shrimp, deveined and tail off (you can use tail on if you prefer)

Coconut cooking spray (regular nonstick cooking spray will also work)

Sweet chili sauce, for dipping, such as Kikkoman or Thai Kitchen

1. In one bowl, whisk together the flour, salt, and pepper. In another bowl, whisk together the coconut and panko. In a third bowl, whisk together the eggs and water.
2. Preheat the air fryer to 375 degrees F. and grease the basket with coconut cooking spray. (Regular non-stick cooking spray will also work.) Line a half-sheet baking pan with parchment paper.
3. A handful at a time, coat the shrimp in the flour mixture and then dip in the egg mixture. Finally, coat the shrimp in the coconut mixture. Arrange the breaded shrimp in a single layer on the prepared baking sheet. Repeat with the remaining shrimp.
4. Add the shrimp to the basket of the preheated air fryer in a single layer, being careful not to crowd the basket. If you need to fry in batches, do so. Air fry for 5 minutes, flip, and air fry for another 5 minutes.
5. Serve hot with sweet chili sauce or your favorite dipping sauce.

SEAFOOD DISHES

Baked Salmon

The simplest salmon recipe, seasoned to perfection with pantry staples, fresh lemon juice, and freshly chopped parsley.

Prep time: 5 min | Cook time: 15 min | Total time: 20 min | Serves 4

---

4 (6-ounce) salmon fillets

2 tablespoons olive oil

2 teaspoons salt

1 teaspoon ground black pepper

1 teaspoon garlic powder

Juice of 2 lemons, divided

4 tablespoons fresh, chopped parsley

1. Preheat the oven to 400 degrees F. and line a half-sheet baking pan with parchment paper.
2. Gently rub the salmon with olive oil, salt, pepper, and garlic powder.
3. Arrange the salmon fillets in a single layer on the prepared baking sheet and squeeze the juice of one lemon over them. Bake for 12–15 minutes or until the flesh of the salmon is flaky but still slightly glassy when pulled apart with a fork. Check the fillets after 12 minutes and give them more time if needed.
4. Squeeze the second lemon over the salmon fillets and sprinkle with parsley. Serve hot.

Lemon Garlic Shrimp Pasta

With tender shrimp tossed in a light, garlicky sauce served over pasta, this is a simple, refreshing meal that's great for any day of the week.

Prep time: 5 min | Cook time: 20 min | Total time: 25 min | Serves 6

8 ounces spaghetti pasta

2 tablespoons butter

2 tablespoons finely chopped onion

4 cloves garlic, minced

¼ cup chicken broth

Juice of 1 lemon

Zest of 1 lemon

½ cup heavy cream

Salt and pepper, to taste

1 pound medium uncooked shrimp, peeled and deveined

4 large basil leaves, chopped

½ cup grated Parmesan cheese

Red pepper flakes, optional for serving

1. Bring a large pot of water to a boil, adding a generous amount of salt. Cook spaghetti al dente as directed on the package, then drain and set aside. Reserve ½ cup of the pasta water.

2. In a separate large skillet, melt butter over medium heat, add in the onion, and sauté for about 2 minutes.

3. Add the garlic, and cook until fragrant, about 1 minute. Add the chicken broth, lemon juice, lemon zest, cream, salt, and pepper. Cook until it starts to simmer, then add shrimp to the skillet and cook until heated through and pink, about 5 minutes.

4. Stir in basil and Parmesan, then toss the cooked spaghetti with the sauce. Add in 1–2 tablespoons of reserved pasta water to loosen the sauce if needed. Top with a sprinkle of pepper flakes if desired, and serve immediately.

Multicooker Salmon Bowls

This quick, healthy meal is perfect for busy weeknights. With tender salmon served over fluffy quinoa and fresh veggies, this Mediterranean-inspired dish is delicious!

Prep time: 5 min | Cook time: 20 min | Pressurize time: 10 min | Total time: 35 min | Serves 4

SALMON

4 (4-ounce) salmon fillets

1 teaspoon salt

½ teaspoon pepper

1 teaspoon garlic powder

1 teaspoon oregano

QUINOA

1 cup quinoa

2 cups water

½ teaspoon salt

1 teaspoon olive oil

TOPPINGS

2 cups toasted chickpeas

1 cucumber, diced

1½ cups halved cherry tomatoes

1 cup pitted kalamata olives

1 cup hummus

¾ cup crumbled feta cheese

½ cup chopped fresh parsley

1. Season the salmon fillets with salt, pepper, garlic powder, and oregano.
2. Place the salmon fillets skin-side-down on top of a trivet in the multicooker. Set the pressure valve to SEAL, and cook on high pressure for 3 minutes. When the timer sounds, set the pressure valve to VENT to perform a manual release.
3. While the salmon is cooking, rinse the quinoa under cold water, then combine the quinoa, water, salt, and olive oil in a medium saucepan. Bring the water to a boil, then reduce the heat to low and cover and simmer for 15 minutes. Remove from the heat, uncover, and fluff the quinoa with a fork.

4. When the salmon and quinoa are finished cooking, divide the quinoa between 4 bowls. Divide the toasted chickpeas between the bowls. Divide the cucumber, cherry tomatoes, and kalamata olives between the bowls. Lay a salmon fillet on top of each bowl and top with a large dollop of hummus. Sprinkle each serving with feta cheese and garnish with parsley.

Note: If you don't love quinoa, you can use cauliflower rice, brown rice, jasmine rice, or any of your favorite rice options in its place for this delicious meal.

New England Clam Chowder

This classic dish will warm you from the inside out! It's loaded with clams, potatoes, and bacon and tastes best served in a sourdough bread bowl.

Prep time: 10 min | Cook time: 20 min | Total time: 30 min | Serves 8

1 tablespoon butter

2 ribs celery, diced

2 teaspoons minced garlic

1 medium onion, diced

4 (6.5-ounce) cans chopped clams, not drained

1 (10.5-ounce) can cream of mushroom soup

3 medium potatoes, peeled and diced

6 strips bacon, cooked and diced

1½ teaspoons dried basil

1½ teaspoons dried thyme

1 bay leaf

Salt and pepper, to taste

3 cups half-and-half

Oyster crackers for serving

1. In a large saucepot over medium heat, melt butter and sauté celery, garlic, and onion until vegetables have softened, about 5 minutes.
2. Add clams (including juice), cream of mushroom soup, potatoes, bacon, basil, thyme, bay leaf, salt and pepper to the pot.
3. Mix thoroughly until combined.
4. Cover and let simmer until potatoes are tender, about 15–20 minutes.
5. Add half-and-half and stir until heated through.
6. Remove bay leaf before serving. We love this topped with oyster crackers.

Note: For thicker or thinner soup, you can add in more or less half-and-half, or add in chicken broth.

Pan-Seared Mahi-Mahi

Seasoned to perfection and flaky on the inside, this restaurant-quality fish dish makes us feel like we're on vacation!

Prep time: 5 min | Cook time: 9 min | Total time: 14 min | Serves 4

1½ teaspoons paprika

½ teaspoon garlic powder

½ teaspoon onion powder

½ teaspoon salt

¼ teaspoon black pepper

1 pinch cayenne pepper

3 tablespoons olive oil

2 tablespoons lemon juice, divided

4 (4-ounce) mahi-mahi fillets

1. In a small bowl, mix together paprika, garlic powder, onion powder, salt, black pepper, cayenne pepper, olive oil, and 1 tablespoon lemon juice.
2. Pat the mahi-mahi dry with paper towels, then brush on the paprika mixture.
3. In a large nonstick skillet, heat oil mixture over medium-high heat. Add the mahi-mahi and sear until browned on the bottom and the sides are cooked about halfway up the fillet, about 4–5 minutes. Flip the fillets and continue to sear until the fish is cooked through to 145 degrees F. and flakes easily, about 3–4 more minutes. Serve immediately, with the remaining lemon juice drizzled over the top.

Note: This pairs great with the Pineapple Mango Salsa on page 192.

Parmesan Fish Sticks with Tartar Sauce

The fish sticks of our childhood get a glow up with these crispy, baked strips of flaky, flavorful tilapia! They get a five-star rating from us dipped in homemade tartar sauce.

Prep time: 20 min | Cook time: 10 min | Total time: 30 min | Serves 4

TARTAR SAUCE

½ cup mayonnaise
¼ cup Greek yogurt
1½ teaspoons pickle juice
½ teaspoon Worcestershire sauce

2¼ teaspoons lemon juice
2 tablespoons chopped fresh dill
2 tablespoons minced dill pickle
Salt and pepper, to taste

FISH STICKS

⅓ cup flour
½ teaspoon salt
¼ teaspoon pepper
2 large eggs
1 cup panko breadcrumbs
⅓ cup grated Parmesan cheese

½ teaspoon garlic powder
½ teaspoon Italian seasoning
1 pound tilapia fillets
Nonstick cooking spray
Freshly squeezed lemon juice, optional topping

1. For the tartar sauce, whisk together the mayo, Greek yogurt, pickle juice, Worcestershire sauce, lemon juice, and dill. Stir in the minced pickle. Taste the tartar sauce and season with salt and pepper as needed. Cover and let rest in the fridge until ready to serve.
2. Preheat the oven to 450 degrees F. Spray a half-sheet baking pan with cooking spray and set aside.
3. In a shallow bowl, mix together flour, salt, and pepper. In another shallow bowl, whisk together eggs. In a third shallow bowl, mix together breadcrumbs, Parmesan cheese, garlic powder, and Italian seasoning.

4. Cut the fillets into inch-wide strips. Dip each strip in flour, shaking off the excess, then dredge in the egg mixture, and finally dip in the panko mixture, patting lightly to make sure it sticks.
5. Place on prepared baking sheet and spray lightly with cooking spray, then bake for 10–12 minutes until golden brown, cooked through, and the fish flakes easily. Squeeze fresh lemon juice over top if desired.
6. Serve with tartar sauce for dipping.

Note: You can also substitute cod, catfish, or any other white fish for the tilapia in this recipe.

Sheet-Pan Shrimp Fajitas

Made in just one pan, these quick and easy fajitas taste delicious served with warm tortillas, cilantro, avocado, and sour cream.

Prep time: 15 min | Cook time: 15 min | Total time: 30 min | Serves 6

1 (1-ounce) package fajita seasoning

3 tablespoons olive oil

2 teaspoons minced garlic

1½ pounds medium uncooked shrimp, peeled and deveined

1 red bell pepper, sliced into strips

1 green bell pepper, sliced into strips

1 yellow bell pepper, sliced into strips

½ yellow onion, sliced into strips

12 (8-inch) tortillas

Diced jalapeño, for topping

Cilantro, for topping

Lime juice, for topping

Sliced avocado, for topping

Sour cream, for topping

1. Preheat the oven to 450 degrees F.
2. Mix fajita seasoning, olive oil, and garlic together in a large bowl. Add shrimp, peppers, and onion to the bowl and toss to coat.
3. Evenly spread shrimp, peppers, and onions in a single layer on a half-sheet baking pan.
4. Bake until the shrimp is cooked through, about 6–8 minutes. Remove the shrimp from the pan and set aside.
5. Place tortillas on a microwave-safe plate or on a damp paper towel in the bottom of a microwave-safe tortilla warmer. Cover with a damp cloth or paper towel. Microwave for 30 seconds.
6. Set the oven to broil, return the pan to the oven, and cook peppers and onions until they begin to char, about 2 to 3 minutes. Remove from the oven and serve immediately with the shrimp, spooning the mixture into warm tortillas and adding preferred toppings.

Turkey Dishes

Egg Roll in a Bowl 139

Honey Garlic Glazed
    Turkey Meatballs 140

Multicooker Ground Turkey
    Taco Chili 143

Multicooker Ground Turkey
    Teriyaki Rice Bowls 144

Quick Italian Turkey Soup 147

Tex-Mex Turkey and
    Rice Skillet 148

Tomato Macaroni Soup 150

Tropical Teriyaki
    Turkey Burgers 153

Turkey Enchiladas 154

Egg Roll in a Bowl

All the egg roll flavors you love—ground turkey, rice vinegar, cabbage, and sesame—no wrapping necessary.

Prep time: 10 min | Cook time: 20 min | Total time: 30 min | Serves 4

2 tablespoons sesame oil

2 tablespoons olive oil

1 tablespoon rice wine vinegar

1 tablespoon less sodium soy sauce

1 teaspoon minced garlic

1 (16-ounce) package ground turkey

½ teaspoon pepper

1 (14–16-ounce) bag shredded coleslaw

8 green onions, chopped

1. In a saucepan over low heat, mix together the sesame oil, olive oil, rice wine vinegar, less sodium soy sauce, and garlic. Whisk until combined.
2. Add ground turkey and let it brown and cook completely through in the sauce mixture.
3. Sprinkle pepper over the meat and sauce mixture.
4. Add coleslaw and continue to stir until soft, but not mushy, about 3–4 minutes.
5. Garnish with green onions and serve.

Honey Garlic Glazed Turkey Meatballs

Sweet and savory, these meatballs make a great meal served over rice, or on toothpicks as a tasty game-day appetizer.

Prep time: 10 min | Cook time: 15 min | Total time: 25 min | Serves 8

---

2 eggs

¾ cup milk

1½ cups dry breadcrumbs

½ onion, diced

2 teaspoons salt

1 (2-pound) package ground turkey

Nonstick cooking spray

4 teaspoons minced garlic

1 tablespoon butter

¾ cup ketchup

½ cup honey

3 tablespoons soy sauce

1. Preheat oven to 400 degrees F.
2. In a large mixing bowl, whisk together eggs and milk.
3. Add breadcrumbs, onion, and salt.
4. Add ground turkey and mix until well combined.
5. Shape turkey mixture into 1-inch balls and place on a half-sheet baking pan sprayed with nonstick cooking spray.
6. Bake for 12–15 minutes, or until cooked through.
7. While meatballs are cooking, combine garlic and butter in a saucepan over medium heat until garlic is tender.
8. Whisk in ketchup, honey, and soy sauce. Bring to a boil.
9. Reduce heat. Cover and simmer for 5 minutes.
10. After meatballs are cooked, spoon sauce over meatballs and serve.

Multicooker Ground Turkey Taco Chili

A tasty spin on a classic recipe, this turkey taco chili has an added flavor of ranch that everyone loves.

Prep time: 5 min | Cook time: 10 min | Pressurize time: 10 min | Total time: 25 min | Serves 6

---

1 pound lean ground turkey (80/20 or 85/15 lean ground beef works as well)

1 yellow onion, diced

3 cloves garlic, minced

1 (1-ounce) package taco seasoning

1 (1-ounce) package ranch salad dressing mix

4 cups chicken broth

1 (14.5-ounce) can diced tomatoes, undrained

1 (4-ounce) can diced green chiles

1 (15-ounce) can black beans, drained and rinsed

1 (15-ounce) can corn, drained

1 (16-ounce) can refried beans

Shredded Mexican blend cheese, for garnish

1. Press SAUTÉ on multicooker. When it's heated, add in ground turkey and onion. Cook for about 5 minutes or until ground turkey is no longer pink.
2. Add in garlic, taco seasoning, ranch seasoning, chicken broth, tomatoes, green chiles, black beans, and corn. Mix together.
3. Add in canned refried beans to the top of the mixture one tablespoonful at a time. Do not mix in.
4. Latch multicooker lid. Turn pressure valve to SEAL. Press MANUAL or PRESSURE COOK button and set timer for 5 minutes.
5. When the timer sounds, allow pressure to do a natural release for 5 minutes, then turn the valve to VENT and do a quick release of the remaining pressure.
6. Remove lid and stir the refried beans into the mixture until creamy and smooth.
7. Serve topped with shredded Mexican cheese.

Multicooker Ground Turkey Teriyaki Rice Bowls

The soy sauce, rice vinegar, and brown sugar give this recipe an amazing flavor profile you won't forget.

Prep time: 10 min | Cook time: 8 min | Pressurize time: 10 min | Total time: 28 min | Serves 6

HOMEMADE TERIYAKI SAUCE

¾ cup less sodium soy sauce

⅓ cup water

3 tablespoons rice vinegar

4 tablespoons brown sugar

2 tablespoons sugar

3 cloves garlic, minced

1½ teaspoons ground ginger

1½ tablespoons cornstarch

3 tablespoons water

GROUND TURKEY

1½ tablespoons olive oil

1 onion, diced

2 tablespoons minced garlic

1 (1.5-pound) package ground turkey (ground beef also works)

1 cup finely chopped broccoli

3 large carrots, peeled and grated

½ red bell pepper, diced

½ cup water

Diced green onions, optional topping

Sesame seeds, optional topping

4 cups cooked rice (we love jasmine rice, but white rice or brown rice will also work)

1. Add less sodium soy sauce, water, rice vinegar, brown sugar, sugar, garlic, and ginger into the multicooker.
2. Press the SAUTÉ button and whisk together as it heats up.
3. While waiting, mix together cornstarch and water in a small bowl.
4. As soon as the sauce starts to bubble, add the cornstarch and water to the sauce in the pot. Whisk for a few seconds until the sauce starts to thicken.

5. Using oven mitts, carefully remove the hot multicooker insert, pour the sauce into a bowl, and set aside.

6. Rinse out insert and return to multicooker.

7. Let the pot warm up again (the SAUTÉ function should still be on) and add in olive oil. Then add in onion, garlic, and ground turkey. Cook until the ground turkey is no longer pink, about 5–6 minutes, breaking up the turkey as it cooks.

8. Add in the broccoli, carrots, and red bell pepper and mix.

9. Mix in the teriyaki sauce so everything is coated in sauce.

10. Pour ½ cup water on top, but don't mix in.

11. Latch the multicooker lid and move the pressure valve to SEAL.

12. Press the CANCEL button to turn off the sauté function, then press MANUAL or PRESSURE COOK and set timer for 2 minutes.

13. When the timer sounds, move the valve to VENT to do a quick release of the pressure.

14. Remove the lid and spoon the mixture over rice to serve. Garnish with green onions and sesame seeds if desired.

Quick Italian Turkey Soup

This light soup is still filling—it's loaded with pasta, beans, and a bunch of veggies to keep you warm and feeling great.

Prep time: 10 min | Cook time: 20 min | Total time: 30 min | Serves 6

½ cup dry rotini pasta

1½ tablespoons olive oil

1 small onion, diced

3 cloves garlic, minced

1 (1-pound) package ground turkey

1 tablespoon Italian seasoning

1 teaspoon salt

½ teaspoon pepper

1 (15-ounce) can Italian-style diced tomatoes

1 (15-ounce) can Great Northern white beans, drained and rinsed

1 cup shredded carrots

1 zucchini, thinly sliced

4 cups chicken broth

1 tablespoon dried parsley

1 teaspoon dried oregano

5 cups finely chopped fresh spinach

Freshly grated Parmesan cheese

1. Cook rotini noodles according to the package directions, and set aside when finished.
2. While the noodles are cooking, heat olive oil in a large stockpot over medium-high heat. Add onions, garlic, ground turkey, Italian seasoning, salt, and pepper. Mix together until turkey is completely cooked through.
3. Add canned tomatoes including juice, white beans, carrots, zucchini, broth, parsley, and oregano.
4. Reduce heat to low and simmer for 10–15 minutes, or until carrots and zucchini are cooked.
5. Add the spinach to the turkey and veggie mixture in the stockpot, and stir it all together until the spinach is wilted. Add additional salt and pepper to taste.
6. Add in cooked rotini and stir it all together, then top each serving with Parmesan cheese.

Tex-Mex Turkey and Rice Skillet

A skillet recipe is a full-flavored, better-for-you one-pan meal. With ground turkey, beans, corn, and rice, it's going to fuel your busy weeknights easily.

Prep time: 20 min | Cook time: 13 min | Total time: 33 min | Serves 6

1½ cups uncooked instant brown rice

1 (1-pound) package lean ground turkey

1 onion, chopped

1 garlic clove, minced

1 (15-ounce) can pinto beans, undrained

1 cup beef broth

1 (8-ounce) can tomato sauce

1 (10-ounce) can diced tomatoes and green chiles, such as RO*TEL, undrained

1 (15.25-ounce) can corn, drained

2 teaspoons chili powder

½ teaspoon salt

½ teaspoon cumin

Ground pepper, to taste

½ cup shredded Colby Jack cheese

1. Cook rice according to package directions.
2. While the rice cooks, heat a large skillet over medium heat. Add in the ground turkey, onion, and garlic and cook until the turkey is no longer pink.
3. Stir in the rice, beans, beef broth, tomato sauce, tomatoes, corn, chili powder, salt, cumin, and ground pepper. Let cook over medium heat for 8–10 minutes to let the flavors really come together.
4. Top with shredded cheese and let cook for 2–3 more minutes or until cheese is melted.
5. Garnish with your favorite toppings—tomatoes, shredded lettuce, salsa, sour cream, etc.

Tomato Macaroni Soup

We love this hearty soup! It's a timeless cold-weather staple that tastes great on its own, and even better with a side of grilled cheese.

Prep time: 10 min | Cook time: 20 min | Total time: 30 min | Serves 6

---

1 (16-ounce) package ground turkey

1 onion, diced

3 (14.5-ounce) cans beef broth

1 (14.5-ounce) can diced tomatoes

1 cup ketchup

1 (6-ounce) can tomato paste

1 cup shredded carrots

3 tablespoons steak sauce, such as A.1.

1 tablespoon brown sugar

1 tablespoon Worcestershire sauce

½ teaspoon dried basil

½ teaspoon garlic powder

Salt and pepper, to taste

1½ cups cooked elbow macaroni

1. In a skillet over medium-high heat, cook ground turkey and diced onions until turkey is browned and onions are soft; drain and set aside.
2. In a large stockpot, mix together beef broth, diced tomatoes, ketchup, tomato paste, carrots, steak sauce, brown sugar, Worcestershire, basil, garlic powder, salt, and pepper and cook over medium-high heat.
3. Bring to a boil, then reduce heat to low. Add turkey and onion and simmer for 10 minutes.
4. Mix in cooked macaroni and serve.

Tropical Teriyaki Turkey Burgers

Flavorful patties topped with melty Swiss cheese, grilled pineapple, and teriyaki sauce, these lightened up burgers are a fan favorite.

Prep time: 10 min | Cook time: 10 min | Total time: 20 min | Serves 6

1 (1.5-pound) package lean ground turkey

¾ cup dry breadcrumbs

½ green bell pepper, diced

1 bunch green onions, diced

¾ teaspoon ground ginger

1 (20-ounce) can pineapple slices (reserve juice)

¾ teaspoon salt

6 slices Swiss cheese

⅓ cup teriyaki sauce, such as Kikkoman or San-J

⅓ cup mayonnaise

6 hamburger buns

1. In a mixing bowl, combine turkey, breadcrumbs, green pepper, green onion, ginger, ¼ cup of the reserved juice from the pineapple, and salt.
2. Divide turkey mixture into 6 equal parts and form into patties.
3. Grill or broil patties until cooked through (cooking in a skillet over medium heat will also work). The last few minutes of cooking, grill pineapple slices and melt a slice of Swiss cheese on top of each patty.
4. Spread 1 tablespoon teriyaki sauce and 1 tablespoon light mayonnaise on buns and top with burgers, adding pineapple slices, then serve.

Turkey Enchiladas

Leftovers never tasted so good! We love making these enchiladas after we've made a full turkey and want to use what's left.

Prep time: 10 min | Cook time: 23 min | Total time: 33 min | Serves 8

Nonstick cooking spray

2 cups shredded cooked turkey

½ teaspoon chili powder, optional

2 cups shredded Monterey Jack cheese, divided

8 (8-inch) flour tortillas

3 tablespoons butter

3 tablespoons flour

2 cups chicken broth

1 cup sour cream

1 (4-ounce) can diced green chiles, drained

1 teaspoon dried cilantro

½ teaspoon onion powder

½ teaspoon garlic powder

¼ teaspoon pepper

1. Preheat oven to 350 degrees F. Grease a 9x13 baking pan with nonstick cooking spray.
2. Mix cooked turkey, chili powder (optional), and 1 cup of Monterey Jack cheese together. Roll up in tortillas and place in pan.
3. In a medium saucepan, melt butter, stir in flour and cook 1 minute. Add broth and whisk until smooth. Heat over medium heat until thick and bubbly.
4. Stir in sour cream, chiles, cilantro, onion powder, garlic powder, and pepper. Do not bring this to a boil—you don't want to have curdled sour cream.
5. Pour over enchiladas and top with remaining cheese.
6. Bake 15–20 minutes and then place under a high broil for 3 minutes to brown the cheese.

Side Dishes

BREADS

Cheesy Garlic Bread. 158

Easy Naan 161

Easy Parmesan
   Crescent Rolls 162

Twisted Cheese Breadsticks . . . 165

SALADS

Citrus Berry Salad 166

Grape Salad. 169

Orange Cream Yogurt Salad . . . 170

Piña Colada Fruit Salad 172

Tortellini Pasta Salad 175

SIDES

Air Fryer Parmesan Broccoli . . . 177

Air Fryer Stuffed Peppers 178

Breakfast Potatoes 181

Corn Salsa 182

Cowboy Baked Beans. 185

Crispy Zucchini Fries with
   Creamy BBQ Sauce. 186

Garlic Parmesan
   Mashed Potatoes 188

Garlic Roasted
   Brussels Sprouts. 191

Pineapple Mango Salsa. 192

Roasted Parmesan
   Sweet Potatoes. 194

Super Greens 197

Cheesy Garlic Bread

Nice and crispy on the outside, soft on the inside, topped with the best homemade garlic butter spread and gooey mozzarella cheese.

Prep time: 10 min | Cook time: 20 min | Total time: 30 min | Serves 8

1 loaf French bread

½ cup butter, softened

4 teaspoons minced garlic

1 teaspoon Italian seasoning

2 cups shredded mozzarella cheese

1. Preheat oven to 400 degrees F.
2. Cover a half-sheet baking pan with foil and set aside.
3. Cut French bread in half lengthwise and place cut sides up on baking sheet.
4. In a small mixing bowl, combine softened butter, garlic, and Italian seasoning.
5. Spread half the garlic butter on each half of bread.
6. Sprinkle one cup shredded mozzarella on each half of the bread.
7. Bake for 15–20 minutes or until the cheese begins to turn golden brown.
8. Cut into slices and serve.

Note: If you prefer a softer garlic bread, wrap each half of the bread in foil before baking. This will help the crust and inside of the bread stay soft and avoid getting crisp. If you prefer a crustier garlic bread, bake your garlic bread uncovered and then broil on high for 1–2 minutes after baking.

Easy Naan

You only need 5 simple ingredients—and no yeast!—to make this soft, chewy bread. It pairs per-fectly with the Multicooker Butter Chicken on page 69!

Prep time: 10 min | Cook time: 20 min | Total time: 30 min | Serves 6

1 cup plain Greek yogurt

1 cup self-rising flour

¼ cup melted butter, divided

1 teaspoon garlic salt, optional topping

¼ cup chopped cilantro, optional topping

1. In the bowl of a stand mixer fitted with the dough hook attachment, combine the Greek yogurt and self-rising flour until a dough starts to form. If the dough is dry, add another tablespoon of yogurt. If it's too tacky, add more flour a tablespoon at a time. Continue to knead until the dough comes together. You can also do this step by hand, but it will take about 15 minutes and some muscle.
2. Lightly flour a work surface and roll the dough into a large ball. Cut the dough into 6 equal pieces.
3. Roll out each piece of dough into a circle about ¼-inch thick and 6 inches in diameter.
4. Heat a skillet over medium-high heat and brush the heated skillet with butter or olive oil. Cook naan on each side for about 2 minutes. It should start to bubble up and lightly char.
5. Remove from the skillet, brush with melted butter, garlic salt, and chopped cilantro as desired.
6. Serve warm.

Note: You may need more or less flour depending on your altitude and humidity levels. At higher eleva-tion, you may end up using 1¼ cups of flour. Always start with less and add more as needed.

Easy Parmesan Crescent Rolls

When you're short on time, but still want a tasty roll side dish, these are just the ticket.

Prep time: 8 min | Cook time: 12 min | Total time: 20 min | Makes 8 to 9 rolls

---

2 tablespoons melted butter, divided

1 (8-ounce) package refrigerated crescent roll dough

½ cup shredded Parmesan cheese, divided

Garlic powder, to taste

Italian seasoning, to taste

1. Preheat oven to 350 degrees F.
2. Pour half the melted butter into the bottom of a 8x8 baking pan.
3. On a floured surface, roll out the crescent roll dough and pinch all the seams together so that you have one sheet of dough. You could also use a prepared full sheet of crescent dough from the deli section of your local grocery store if they offer it.
4. Sprinkle half the Parmesan cheese over the dough. Lightly sprinkle garlic powder and Italian seasoning on the dough as desired.
5. Roll up the dough lengthwise into a long, skinny tube and, using a sharp knife, carefully slice it into 1-inch pieces. You should get 8–9 pieces.
6. Place the dough slices into the prepared pan. Using a basting brush, brush remaining butter on top of rolls. Sprinkle remaining Parmesan cheese on top of rolls.
7. Bake for 11–13 minutes or until the tops of the rolls start to turn golden brown.

SIDE DISHES

Twisted Cheese Breadsticks

We use a shortcut on these twisted cheese breadsticks to make them even easier to make quickly—puff pastry! They turn out perfect every time.

Prep time: 15 min | Cook time: 15 min | Total time: 30 min | Serves 12

---

1 (17.3 ounce) package frozen puff pastry, such as Pepperidge Farm

2 tablespoons olive oil

Salt, to taste

Pepper, to taste

Garlic salt, to taste

2 cups shredded mozzarella cheese

1. Preheat oven to 400 degrees F. Line a half-sheet baking pan with parchment paper.
2. Allow dough to thaw on a floured surface. It is thawed enough when you can unfold it.
3. Unfold each sheet and lay flat. Brush with olive oil, and sprinkle with salt, pepper, and garlic salt.
4. Sprinkle 1 cup mozzarella cheese over each sheet, pressing it down firmly into the dough with your fingers.
5. Cut each sheet lengthwise into 1½-inch strips (about 6 strips from each sheet).
6. Twist each strip and set it on the prepared baking pan.
7. Bake for 10–15 minutes, or until cheese is melted and breadsticks start to turn golden.

Citrus Berry Salad

The citrus and berry flavors combine to create a delicious salad that tastes like it came from a restaurant.

Prep time: 15 min | Total time: 15 min | Serves 6

SALAD

12 cups baby spinach leaves

3 clementine oranges, peeled and separated

¾ cup fresh raspberries

¾ cup fresh blackberries

¾ cup sliced fresh strawberries

⅓ cup chopped walnuts

¼ cup feta cheese crumbles

DRESSING

½ cup orange juice

2 tablespoons olive oil

1½ tablespoons balsamic vinegar

¼ cup honey

1. Combine spinach leaves, oranges, raspberries, blackberries, and strawberries in a large bowl.
2. Top salad with chopped walnuts and feta cheese crumbles.
3. In a medium-size bowl, whisk together orange juice, olive oil, balsamic vinegar, and honey until fully incorporated.
4. Pour the salad dressing over the salad before serving and toss to coat.

Grape Salad

This recipe has been around for decades and makes a sweet, creamy side dish perfect for potlucks, picnics, or anytime you're craving more fruit.

Prep time: 10 min | Total time: 10 min | Serves 8

---

2 pounds red seedless grapes

2 pounds green seedless grapes

1 (8-ounce) package cream cheese

1 (8-ounce) container sour cream

½ cup sugar

⅔ cups chopped pecans, divided

½ teaspoon vanilla

¼ cup brown sugar, divided

1. Wash and dry grapes and set aside.
2. In a big bowl, mix cream cheese and sour cream together. Then add sugar, ⅓ cup pecans, and vanilla.
3. Gently stir in ⅛ cup brown sugar.
4. Add the grapes and stir gently until mixed well.
5. Sprinkle with remaining pecans and brown sugar.
6. Refrigerate until ready to serve.

Orange Cream Yogurt Salad

Whether you serve it as a side dish or as a light dessert, this creamy dish made with pudding, juice concentrate, yogurt, and fruit is always a crowd favorite.

Prep time: 10 min | Total time: 10 min | Serves 8

---

1 (3.4-ounce) instant vanilla pudding mix, such as Jell-O

⅓ cup orange juice concentrate, thawed

½ cup milk

1 cup vanilla Greek yogurt

1 (20-ounce) can pineapple tidbits, drained

2 (10-ounce) cans mandarin oranges, drained

2 bananas, sliced

1 cup mini marshmallows

1. In a large bowl, mix together dry pudding mix, orange juice concentrate, and milk using a hand mixer.
2. Mix in yogurt.
3. Add in all remaining ingredients, draining the canned fruits well. If not serving immediately, don't add sliced bananas until you are ready to serve.

Note: Make sure that you drain the pineapple and mandarin oranges *very* well, otherwise this salad tends to get watery.

Piña Colada Fruit Salad

We used a piña colada mix to change up a classic fruit salad, and now we can't stop! Everyone loves this easy side.

Prep time: 15 min | Total time: 15 min | Serves 6

⅓ cup non-alcoholic Piña Colada mix, such as Daily's or Master of Mixes

⅓ cup pineapple juice

½ teaspoon coconut extract

2 cups cubed fresh pineapple

½ cup halved green grapes

½ cup halved red grapes

½ cup blueberries

½ cup raspberries

½ cup blackberries

10 strawberries, quartered

2 clementine oranges, such as Cuties, peeled and sectioned

1. Whisk together the piña colada mix, pineapple juice, and coconut extract and set aside.
2. Toss together the pineapple, grapes, blueberries, raspberries, blackberries, strawberries, and clementines in a large salad bowl. Drizzle the sauce over the fruit and gently toss to coat the fruit evenly in the sauce.
3. Cover and chill in the refrigerator until you're ready to serve.

Tortellini Pasta Salad

Loaded with fresh vegetables, cheesy tortellini, feta cheese crumbles, and a zesty homemade vinaigrette dressing, this easy pasta salad is always a hit.

Prep time: 20 min | Cook time: 10 min | Total time: 30 min | Serves 8

PASTA SALAD

1 (20-ounce) package cheese tortellini

1 orange bell pepper, diced

1 yellow bell pepper, diced

½ red onion, sliced

1 cucumber, diced

1 cup halved cherry tomatoes

½ cup sliced olives

1 cup artichoke hearts

1 (4-ounce) container feta cheese crumbles, such as Litehouse

SALAD DRESSING

¼ cup olive oil

5 tablespoons red wine vinegar

½ teaspoon dried oregano

½ teaspoon black pepper

1 teaspoon sugar

1. Boil a large pot of water and cook the tortellini according to the directions on the package. Once it's done cooking, drain and pour into a large bowl.
2. Fold in peppers, onion, cucumber, tomatoes, olives, artichoke hearts, and feta cheese.
3. Whisk together salad dressing ingredients and pour over salad.
4. Toss salad until dressing is evenly distributed.
5. Cover with plastic wrap and refrigerate until serving.

Air Fryer Parmesan Broccoli

Full of flavor and just the right amount of crispiness, this air fryer broccoli is one of our favorite simple side dishes.

Prep time: 10 min | Cook time: 6 min | Total time: 16 min | Serves 4

---

1 head of broccoli, cut into evenly sized pieces

1 tablespoon olive oil

¼ teaspoon onion powder

¼ teaspoon garlic powder

Salt and pepper, to taste

Pinch crushed red pepper flakes, to taste, optional

1 tablespoon water

Grated Parmesan cheese, optional topping

1. Preheat air fryer to 375 degrees F.
2. In a large bowl, toss broccoli with olive oil, onion powder, garlic powder, salt, pepper, and red pepper flakes, if using.
3. Pour 1 tablespoon water into the bottom of the air fryer. This helps the food not to smoke and burn.
4. Lay the broccoli in a single layer in the bottom of the air fryer basket.
5. Cook until tender and crisp, about 8–10 minutes. Start checking it around 7 minutes—you can always cook it longer if needed.
6. Remove from basket, sprinkle grated Parmesan cheese on top, and serve immediately.

Air Fryer Stuffed Peppers

Filled with taco-seasoned lean meat, rice, and melty cheese, these stuffed peppers are anything but boring. Now you can make them even quicker in your air fryer!

Prep time: 10 min | Cook time: 20 min | Total time: 30 min | Serves 4 (2 halves per person)

---

4 red bell peppers

1 (1-pound) package lean ground turkey

½ cup cooked rice

1 (10-ounce) can diced tomatoes and green chiles, such as RO*TEL, drained

1 (1-ounce) packet less sodium taco seasoning

1 cup shredded cheddar cheese

1. Preheat air fryer to 375 degrees F.
2. Wash peppers and slice in half from top to bottom. Remove all seeds and membranes from the inside.
3. In a large saucepan, brown ground turkey until cooked through.
4. Add rice, diced tomatoes, and taco seasoning to the meat. Mix until combined. Scoop the mixture into peppers, filling each half completely.
5. Place the peppers in the air fryer basket and air fry for 10 minutes. Add cheese and fry for 2–3 minutes more until the cheese is melted. Depending on the size of your air fryer, you may need to repeat this step until all peppers are cooked.
6. Serve immediately.

Breakfast Potatoes

Just the right amount of crispy on the outside and tender on the inside, these potatoes are the perfect breakfast, brunch, or "brinner" side dish.

Prep time: 10 min │ Cook time: 20 min │ Total time: 30 min │ Serves 4

1 tablespoon olive oil

1 tablespoon butter

1 red bell pepper, roughly chopped

½ green bell pepper, chopped

½ red onion, chopped

¾ pounds mini Yukon gold potatoes, washed and quartered

1 teaspoon salt

1 teaspoon garlic powder

1 teaspoon smoked paprika

1. In a large skillet or frying pan, heat the olive oil and butter over medium heat until the butter has melted. Add the bell peppers and onion to the skillet. Sauté until they begin to soften.

2. Add the potatoes to the skillet and season with salt, garlic powder, and smoked paprika.

3. Allow the potatoes to cook without stirring for a few minutes to develop a crispy crust. Flip, then continue to cook, stirring occasionally, for about 15–20 minutes or until the potatoes are tender on the inside and crispy on the outside. You can add a splash of water to the pan occasionally to prevent burning.

Corn Salsa

This dip is a zesty mix of sweet corn, citrus juices, onions, pepper, and cilantro. It's delicious with tortilla chips or on top of nachos, rice bowls, or tacos.

Prep time: 10 min | Total time: 10 min | Serves 8

1 (16-ounce) package frozen white corn (yellow corn also works), completely thawed

2 tablespoons lime juice

1 tablespoon lemon juice

⅓ cup finely diced red onion

1 small jalapeño pepper, seeded and finely diced

1 small poblano pepper, seeded and finely diced

½ cup roughly chopped fresh cilantro

1. Combine all ingredients in a mixing bowl.
2. You can serve immediately or cover and refrigerate for a few hours to let the flavors combine well, then serve.

Cowboy Baked Beans

The heartiest side dish loaded with ground beef, bacon, and two types of beans, these are every BBQ goer's dream.

Prep time: 15 min | Cook time: 10 min | Total time: 25 min | Serves 8

1 (1-pound) package ground beef

1 onion, chopped

¾ pound bacon, cooked and crumbled

2 (15-ounce) cans pork and beans

1 (15.5-ounce) can red kidney beans, drained well

1 cup ketchup

½ cup brown sugar

2 tablespoons liquid smoke

Salt, to taste

1. Brown meat and sauté onion together on medium-high heat in a skillet.
2. After the ground beef is cooked through, drain the grease well.
3. In another skillet, cook bacon, then crumble into small pieces and add to the meat and onion mixture.
4. Stir the remaining ingredients into the large pan and simmer for 10 minutes. Serve warm.

Crispy Zucchini Fries with Creamy BBQ Sauce

Forget deep-fried—these baked zucchini fries are a kid favorite. With a crispy cheese coating and a tangy sauce, we know you'll love this fun side.

Prep time: 10 min | Cook time: 20 min | Total time: 30 min | Serves 6

ZUCCHINI FRIES

Nonstick cooking spray

2 large eggs

3 tablespoons flour

½ cup breadcrumbs

¼ teaspoon garlic powder

2 tablespoons grated Parmesan cheese

Salt and pepper, to taste

3 medium zucchini, cut into thin sticks

CREAMY BBQ SAUCE

½ cup barbecue sauce, such as Sweet Baby Ray's

½ cup mayonnaise

1. Preheat oven to 425 degrees F. Spray a half-sheet baking pan with nonstick cooking spray and set aside.
2. In a small bowl, beat eggs with a fork until well combined.
3. Add the flour to another small bowl.
4. Fill a third bowl with breadcrumbs. Toss the breadcrumbs with garlic powder and Parmesan cheese, add salt and pepper to taste, then set aside.
5. Dip the zucchini sticks into the flour and shake off the extra, then dip in beaten egg, then into the breadcrumb mixture. Make sure all sides get coated well. Place the sticks on the prepared baking sheet.
6. Bake for about 20 minutes or until golden brown and crispy.
7. Mix the barbecue sauce and mayo and serve in a separate dish for dipping.

Garlic Parmesan Mashed Potatoes

The quintessential side dish made even more flavorful and creamy. Did we mention they go with pretty much everything?

Prep time: 10 min | Cook time: 20 min | Total time: 30 min | Serves 10

5 pounds red potatoes, washed and diced

1 tablespoon salt

6 teaspoons minced garlic

1½–2 cups low-fat milk

½ cup grated Parmesan cheese

1. Place potatoes in a large pot, add salt, and cover with water.
2. Bring to a boil over medium-high heat and cook until potatoes are tender, about 20 minutes.
3. Remove the potatoes from heat and drain the water.
4. Mash the potatoes and add the garlic and milk gradually. Mash using an electric hand mixer for smoother potatoes or a potato masher for chunkier potatoes.
5. Add Parmesan cheese and mix until combined, then serve.

Garlic Roasted Brussels Sprouts

This is the best way to make crispy Brussels sprouts with fresh garlic and a handful of other pantry staples.

Prep time: 10 min | Cook time: 20 min | Total time: 30 min | Serves 4

---

2 pounds Brussels sprouts, halved lengthwise and ends cut off

3 garlic cloves, thinly sliced

2 tablespoons olive oil

½ teaspoon sea salt

¼ teaspoon ground black pepper

1. Preheat the oven to 425 degrees F. and line a half-sheet baking pan with aluminum foil.
2. In a large mixing bowl, combine the halved Brussels sprouts, garlic, olive oil, salt, and pepper. Toss to coat the sprouts in olive oil and seasoning.
3. Spread the Brussels sprouts over the prepared pan and bake for 20–25 minutes or until softened and golden brown.

Pineapple Mango Salsa

This sweet, tangy, slightly spicy salsa pairs with just about anything—atop fresh fish, with your favorite tacos, or just with tortilla chips.

Prep time: 10 min | Total time: 10 min | Serves 6

1 mango, peeled and chopped

1 cup drained pineapple tidbits

1 Roma tomato

1 tablespoon finely chopped cilantro

2 green onions, sliced

2 tablespoons lime juice

1 tablespoon lemon juice

1 jalapeño pepper, ribs and seeds removed and finely diced

1. Mix all ingredients together in a bowl. Store covered in the refrigerator until ready to serve.

Roasted Parmesan Sweet Potatoes

We love a good sweet potato side, and this is one of the best. Diced and tossed with spices and cheese, they're simple yet satisfying.

Prep time: 15 min | Cook time: 15 min | Total time: 30 min | Serves 5

Nonstick baking spray

1½–2 pounds sweet potatoes, peeled and diced into bite-size pieces about 1 inch square

3 tablespoons olive oil

¼ cup grated Parmesan cheese

1½ teaspoons paprika

¾ teaspoon garlic powder

½ teaspoon salt

¼ teaspoon pepper

1. Preheat oven to 425 degrees F.
2. Line a half-sheet baking pan with aluminum foil and spray with nonstick cooking spray.
3. Dump diced potatoes on the foil-lined pan.
4. Drizzle olive oil over the potatoes and, using your hands, gently toss the potatoes until oil has covered all the potatoes.
5. In a small bowl, mix together the Parmesan cheese, paprika, garlic powder, salt, and pepper. Sprinkle over the potatoes and, once again, use your hands to incorporate spices over the potatoes.
6. Bake for 15–18 minutes, or until the potatoes reach desired softness, stirring halfway through so they're evenly cooked and don't get burned on the bottom.
7. When finished baking, remove from oven and sprinkle with additional salt and pepper, if desired.

Super Greens

This side dish is a copycat of one of our favorite chain restaurant's dishes and pairs perfectly with any Asian-inspired main dish!

Prep time: 5 min | Cook time: 10 min | Total time: 15 min | Serves 6

1 tablespoon butter

1 tablespoon toasted sesame oil

1½ tablespoons fresh grated ginger

2 garlic cloves, minced

3 tablespoons less sodium soy sauce

4 cups bite-size broccoli pieces

½ head green cabbage, roughly chopped

4 cups roughly chopped kale

¼ cup vegetable stock or water

2 tablespoons sesame seeds, for garnish

1. In a large skillet over medium-high heat, melt the butter. Add the sesame oil, ginger, and garlic and sauté until aromatic. Whisk in the soy sauce.
2. Add the broccoli to the skillet followed by the cabbage and the kale. Pour the water over the veggies and put a lid on the skillet. Cook for 5 minutes or until the broccoli is fork-tender, stirring every couple of minutes.
3. Serve warm, garnished with sesame seeds.

Desserts

Cake Mix
Peanut Butter Bars 201

Chewy Homemade
M&M's Cookies 202

Cinnamon Twists 205

Lemon Blueberry Trifle 206

Lemon Brownies with
Lemon Frosting 208

Lemon Cheesecake
Pudding Cookies 211

Mango Pineapple
Frozen Whip 212

PB&J Thumbprint Cookies 215

Puff Pastry Donuts........... 216

Red Velvet Whoopie Pie
Sandwich Cookies 219

S'mores Clusters.............220

White Chocolate
Cinnamon Sugar Pretzels 223

Cake Mix Peanut Butter Bars

You need only a few ingredients to make this easy bar recipe. The soft, peanut butter base with smooth chocolate frosting is a match made in heaven.

Prep time: 10 min | Cook time: 20 min | Total time: 30 min | Makes 24 bars

BARS

Nonstick cooking spray

1 cup peanut butter

½ cup water

1 large egg

1 (13.25-ounce) boxed yellow cake mix

FROSTING

½ cup margarine, softened

¼ cup milk

2 teaspoons vanilla extract

3 tablespoons cocoa powder

3 cups powdered sugar

1. Preheat the oven to 350 degrees F.
2. Spray a 9x13 baking pan with nonstick cooking spray and set aside.
3. In a medium bowl, combine peanut butter, water, and egg, stirring until smooth. Stir in cake mix until well blended. Spread into prepared pan.
4. Bake 20 to 25 minutes or until puffed and light golden brown. Allow to cool completely.
5. For frosting, mix all ingredients with an electric hand mixer until smooth. Add more powdered sugar or milk until you reach the desired consistency. Spread on top of cooled bars.

Chewy Homemade M&M's Cookies

A classic cookie recipe that's a must-have for every kitchen, these soft, chewy M&M's cookies are never a bad idea.

Prep time: 10 min | Cook time: 11 min | Total time: 21 min | Makes 24 cookies

---

1 cup packed brown sugar

½ cup white sugar

1 cup butter, room temperature

2 eggs

1½ teaspoons vanilla extract

2½ cups flour

1 teaspoon baking soda

1 teaspoon salt

1½ cups candy-coated milk chocolate pieces, such as M&M's, divided

1. Preheat oven to 350 degrees F.
2. In a large bowl, mix sugars, butter, eggs, and vanilla thoroughly. Add flour, baking soda, and salt to creamed mixture. Blend well. Add ¾ cup candies. Drop dough by teaspoonful onto an ungreased cookie sheet. Using remaining candies, slightly push a few candies into each dough ball.
3. Bake for 9 to 11 minutes, or until slightly golden.

Cinnamon Twists

If you love a good copycat recipe, then you need to try these copycat cinnamon twists! They're perfectly crunchy and delicious.

Prep time: 15 min | Cook time: 10 min | Total time: 25 min | Makes 2 cups of twists

1 quart canola oil

½ cup granulated sugar

2 tablespoons cinnamon

1 (16-ounce) package Mexican wheat pellet twists, such as Duros

1. Clip a candy thermometer onto a 2-quart saucepan so that its sensor hits the bottom of the inside wall of the pan. Fill the saucepan halfway with canola oil. Heat over medium heat on the stovetop until the candy thermometer reads 350 degrees F. Reduce the heat to medium-low. While the oil is heating, set a wire rack over a half-sheet baking pan near the stove.
2. Next to the wire rack, place a large mixing bowl. Fill the mixing bowl with the sugar and cinnamon and mix together.
3. Gently scoop 1 cup of Duros into the hot oil. They will sink to the bottom of the saucepan and remain unchanged for a few seconds. Then, they will suddenly puff up and float to the top of the oil. Once all of the Duros reach the top of the oil—this will happen fast—count to 20, flipping them occasionally, before scooping them out with a spider skimmer and spreading them over the wire rack.
4. Give the oil a few seconds to drain from the fried Duros. Once cool enough to handle, transfer the fried twists to the bowl with cinnamon sugar and toss to coat. Transfer to a large serving bowl.
5. Repeat steps 3 and 4 twice, frying 1 cup of Duros per batch.

Lemon Blueberry Trifle

We love a beautiful, tasty dessert, and this Lemon Blueberry Trifle is just that! Layers of angel food cake, pudding, and fresh blueberries make this tart dessert perfect for warm weather.

Prep time: 20 min | Total time: 20 min | Serves 12

2 (8-ounce) packages cream cheese, softened

1 (8-ounce) tub whipped topping, such as Cool Whip

1 cup powdered sugar

2 loaves angel food cake, cut into cubes

2 cups blueberries

2 (3.4-ounce) boxes instant lemon pudding, such as Jell-O

6 cups milk

1. In a large bowl, combine cream cheese, whipped topping, and powdered sugar until fully combined and smooth.
2. In your trifle dish, start by layering the cake on the bottom, place half the cream cheese mixture on top of the cake and smooth out until fully covering the cake layer.
3. Prepare the pudding according to the box instructions.
4. Spread half the lemon pudding on top of the cream cheese layer until all the white is covered.
5. Place about half the blueberries on top of the pudding.
6. Repeat the layering process.
7. Garnish with extra blueberries.
8. Refrigerate until ready to serve.

Lemon Brownies with Lemon Frosting

If lemon bars and fudgy brownies got together, they would make these lemon brownies, a must-make for all of the lemon lovers out there.

Prep time: 10 min | Cook time: 20 min | Total time: 30 min | Makes 15 brownies

LEMON BROWNIES

Nonstick cooking spray

2 (8-ounce) sticks salted butter, at room temperature

1½ cups sugar

4 room temperature eggs

½ cup lemon juice (the juice of about 4 lemons)

Dash vanilla extract

2 cups all-purpose flour

1 teaspoon baking powder

Pinch salt

2 tablespoons fresh lemon zest

FROSTING

¼ cup butter

4 ounces cream cheese

3 tablespoons fresh lemon juice

⅔ cup powdered sugar

1 tablespoon fresh lemon zest to garnish

1. Preheat the oven to 350 degrees F. and grease a 9x13 baking dish with nonstick cooking spray.
2. In the bowl of a stand-up mixer fitted with the paddle attachment, cream together the butter and sugar on high speed.
3. Add the eggs one at a time, mixing between each addition.
4. Add the lemon juice and vanilla extract and mix to combine.
5. Right on top of the wet ingredients, add the all-purpose flour, baking powder, salt, and fresh lemon zest. Mix on low speed until combined. Do not overmix.
6. Pour the batter into the prepared baking dish, smooth with a rubber spatula, and bake for 20 minutes or until a toothpick inserted into the center comes out clean.
7. Allow to cool for 5–10 minutes before transferring to a wire rack and cooling completely.

8. To make the frosting, cream together the butter, cream cheese, and lemon juice on medium-high speed until smooth. Add the powdered sugar and mix on low speed until incorporated. Spread the frosting over the cooled lemon brownies and sprinkle with lemon zest.

Lemon Cheesecake Pudding Cookies

These soft, chewy cookies are bursting with lemon flavor. We bet you can't eat just one!

Prep time: 15 min | Cook time: 10 min | Total time: 25 min | Makes 30 cookies

---

3 ounces cream cheese, softened

¼ cup shortening

2 eggs

1 cup sugar

6 tablespoons salted butter, melted

1 (3.4-ounce) box instant lemon pudding mix

½ teaspoon almond extract

¾ teaspoon baking soda

½ teaspoon baking powder

½ teaspoon salt

1¾ cups all-purpose flour

1 cup white chocolate chips

1. Preheat oven to 350 degrees F. and line half-sheet baking pans with parchment paper or silicone baking mats. Set aside.
2. Add softened cream cheese, shortening, eggs, and sugar to the bowl of a stand mixer or large mixing bowl. Cream together for one minute. Add melted butter and pudding mix and stir for an additional minute. Add almond extract and mix until combined.
3. In a smaller separate mixing bowl, sift together baking soda, baking powder, salt, and flour. Add dry mix to wet ingredients and mix until completely combined.
4. Fold in white chocolate chips.
5. Place spoonfuls of dough on prepared baking sheets and bake for 8–10 minutes until tops and edges start to turn golden brown and cookies are lightly set. Allow to cool on pan for 3–5 minutes before transferring to cooling racks. Allow to completely cool before serving.

Mango Pineapple Frozen Whip

This dairy-free dessert is reminiscent of the many flavors of frozen fruit whip you can find at Disney resorts. We love the delicious mango pineapple flavors combined with coconut cream.

Prep time: 10 min | Total time: 10 min | Serves 4

¼ cup coconut cream solids

1 cup frozen pineapples

1 cup frozen mangoes

2 tablespoons honey

1 teaspoon lemon juice

Pinch of salt

1. Refrigerate a 13.5-ounce can of coconut cream overnight. Open the can and remove the solids that have risen to the top of the can and measure ¼ cup.
2. Combine the coconut cream, frozen pineapples, frozen mangos, honey, lemon juice, and salt in a blender and blend until smooth.
3. Scoop the whip into a piping bag and swirl it into bowls. Top with fresh fruit.

Note: If you would like a more frozen dessert, tie a filled piping bag with a rubber band and keep it in the freezer for 30 minutes before piping it into bowls.

PB&J Thumbprint Cookies

Only 5 ingredients needed to turn your favorite sandwiches into scrumptious little thumbprint cookies.

Prep time: 15 min | **Cook time:** 12 min | **Total time:** 27 min | **Makes 24 small cookies**

---

1 cup sugar

1 cup creamy peanut butter

1 egg

2 teaspoons vanilla extract

1 (10-ounce or half-pint) jar raspberry jam
(or other homemade jam)

1. Preheat oven to 350 degrees F.
2. In a mixing bowl, combine sugar, peanut butter, egg, and vanilla extract.
3. Line a cookie sheet with a silicone liner or parchment paper. Roll tablespoon-sized portions of dough into balls and drop onto prepared cookie sheet.
4. Using the back of a tablespoon or your thumb, make an indentation in each cookie. Fill each indent with raspberry or other favorite jam.
5. Bake for 11–12 minutes, then remove from oven and place on a wire rack to finish cooling.

Puff Pastry Donuts

No donut pan or deep fryer needed to make these melt-in-your-mouth glazed donuts.

Prep time: 10 min | Cook time: 10 min | Total time: 20 min | Makes 24 donuts

---

2 sheets puff pastry, thawed

Vegetable oil for frying

2 cups powdered sugar

4 tablespoons milk

2 teaspoons vanilla extract

1. On a lightly floured surface, roll out puff pastry.
2. Cut circles out of puff pastry in a donut shape using a larger circle cookie cutter for the outside and a smaller circle cookie cutter for the center.
3. Fill a large saucepan or high-sided skillet with an inch of vegetable oil and heat over medium-high heat.
4. Cook donuts in hot vegetable oil, flipping when one side is golden.
5. In a mixing bowl, whisk together powdered sugar, milk, and vanilla to make glaze.
6. Dip the still-hot donuts in the glaze using tongs or a slotted spoon.

Red Velvet Whoopie Pie Sandwich Cookies

These cookies are so easy to make using a cake mix shortcut! They turn out soft, chewy, and delicious every time.

Prep time: 20 min | Cook time: 10 min | Total time: 30 min | Makes 15 sandwich cookies

COOKIES

1 (15.25-ounce) boxed red velvet cake mix

2 eggs, lightly beaten

½ cup vegetable oil

FROSTING

1 (8-ounce) package cream cheese, softened

¼ cup butter, softened

2 teaspoons milk

1 teaspoon vanilla

3 cups powdered sugar (more or less for consistency)

1. Preheat the oven to 375 degrees F.
2. Mix together the cake mix, eggs, and oil in a large bowl. Roll the dough into balls the size of walnuts. Place 2 inches apart on ungreased baking sheets.
3. Bake until the tops start to crack, about 8 minutes. Allow to cool in the pan for 10 minutes before removing to cool completely on a wire rack.
4. In a large bowl, combine cream cheese, butter, milk, and vanilla. Add the powdered sugar 1 cup at a time, mixing well with each addition. If the consistency is too stiff, add more milk.
5. Spread a generous amount of icing on the bottom of a cookie, sandwich it with another cookie, pressing firmly so that the icing comes all the way out to the edge. Repeat with the remaining cookies.

S'mores Clusters

This is the best way to enjoy indoor s'mores. Fluffy marshmallows, graham cracker crunch, all covered in chocolate with a lot less mess—and no fire necessary.

Prep time: 10 min | Cooling time: 20 min | Total time: 30 min | Makes 15 clusters

---

1 (12-ounce) package milk chocolate chips

1½ teaspoons vegetable oil

1½ cups crushed graham crackers

2 cups mini marshmallows

1. Line a half-sheet baking pan with wax paper and set aside.
2. In a microwave-safe bowl, melt together chocolate chips and vegetable oil in 30-second intervals, stirring in between each interval, until smooth.
3. Stir in crushed graham crackers and mini marshmallows, completely coating them in chocolate.
4. Drop by large spoonfuls onto the prepared baking pan and allow to cool and set up, about 20 minutes, then serve.

White Chocolate Cinnamon Sugar Pretzels

Pretzels covered in cinnamon sugar, then drizzled in white chocolate. They're the perfect snack or dessert when you need something sweet, salty, and crunchy.

Prep time: 15 min | Total time: 15 min | Serves 12

⅔ cup vegetable oil

⅓ cup sugar

1½ teaspoons cinnamon

1 (16-ounce) bag pretzels

Cinnamon sugar (½ cup granulated sugar mixed with 2 tablespoons cinnamon), for sprinkling

1 cup white chocolate chips

1. Whisk together oil, sugar, and cinnamon.
2. Pour pretzels into a microwave-safe bowl and pour oil mixture in. Stir until coated.
3. Microwave for 1 minute, remove and stir. Microwave 45 seconds more.
4. Spread pretzels evenly onto two cookie sheets covered in parchment paper. While still warm, sprinkle cinnamon sugar generously.
5. Melt white chocolate in a small saucepan on low heat, being careful not to burn, and drizzle over cooled pretzels.
6. Store in an airtight container.

Index

Page numbers in **bold** *refer to photos*

A
Air Fryer Buffalo Chicken Wings, **50**, 51
Air Fryer Chicken Breasts, Perfect, 70, **71**
Air Fryer Chicken Tenders, 52, **53**
Air Fryer Coconut Shrimp, **120**, 121
Air Fryer Cube Steak with Gravy, 26–27, **27**
Air Fryer Parmesan Broccoli, **176**, 177
Air Fryer Parmesan Spinach Stuffed Mushrooms, 2, **3**
Air Fryer Pizzas, **94**, 95
Air Fryer Stuffed Peppers, 178, **179**
Alfredo, Fettuccine, 80, **81**
Appetizers, 1–23
  Air Fryer Parmesan Spinach Stuffed Mushrooms, 2, **3**
  Bacon-Wrapped Tater Tots with Dipping Sauce, **4**, 5
  Buffalo Ranch Deviled Eggs, 6, **7**
  Chicken Taco Roll-Ups, 8, **9**
  Green Goddess Vegetable Dip, **14**, 15
  Million-Dollar Dip, **16**, 17
  Multicooker Spinach Artichoke Dip, 18, **19**
  Queso Blanco Dip, **20**, 21
  Twisted Pretzel Bites, **10**, 11
  Warm Bacon Cheese Dip, **22**, 23
  Zucchini Feta Bruschetta, 12, **13**
Apricot Chicken, Multicooker, **66**, 67

Artichoke hearts
  Multicooker Spinach Artichoke Dip, 18, **19**
  Tortellini Pasta Salad, **174**, 175
Asian-Inspired Beef and Snow Peas, **28**, 29
Avocados. *See also* Guacamole
  Chicken Taco Roll-Ups, 8, **9**
  Crispy Bean and Cheese Burritos, **78**, 79
  Mexican Street Corn Chicken Tacos, 64–65, **65**
  Sheet-Pan Shrimp Fajitas, **134**, 135

B
Bacon
  Bacon Ranch Chicken, **54**, 55
  Bacon-Wrapped Tater Tots with Dipping Sauce, **4**, 5
  Chicken Bacon Alfredo French Bread Pizza, **62**, 63
  Cowboy Baked Beans, **184**, 185
  Million-Dollar Dip, **16**, 17
  Multicooker Loaded Mac and Cheese, 108, **109**
  New England Clam Chowder, 128, **129**
  Warm Bacon Cheese Dip, **22**, 23
Bacon Cheese Dip, Warm, **22**, 23
Bacon Ranch Chicken, **54**, 55
Bacon-Wrapped Tater Tots with Dipping Sauce, **4**, 5
Baked Beans, Cowboy, **184**, 185
Baked Creamy Chicken Taquitos, 56, **57**

Baked Ham and Cheese Croissant Sandwiches, 96, **97**
Baked Salmon, 122, **123**
BBQ Chicken and Pineapple Quesadillas, **58**, 59
BBQ Sloppy Joes, 30, **31**
Bean and Cheese Burritos, Crispy, **78**, 79
Beans
  Cowboy Baked Beans, **184**, 185
  Crispy Bean and Cheese Burritos, **78**, 79
  Fiesta Ground Beef Enchiladas, **38**, 39
  Ground Beef Quesadillas, 42, **43**
  Multicooker Ground Turkey Taco Chili, **142**, 143
  Oven-Baked Beef Tacos, 46, **47**
  Quick Italian Turkey Soup, **146**, 147
  Seven-Layer Dip Burritos, 84, **85**
  Tex-Mex Turkey and Rice Skillet, 148, **149**
  Tuscan White Bean Soup, 116, **117**
Beef and Snow Peas, Asian-Inspired, **28**, 29
Beef dishes, 25–47. *See also* Ground beef
  Air Fryer Cube Steak with Gravy, 26–27, **27**
  Asian-Inspired Beef and Snow Peas, **28**, 29
  BBQ Sloppy Joes, 30, **31**
  Chopped Cheese Sandwich, **32**, 33
  Classic Burgers, 34, **35**

Creamy Beef and Tomato Pasta, 36, **37**

Fiesta Ground Beef Enchiladas, **38**, 39

Grilled Teriyaki Burgers, **40**, 41

Ground Beef Quesadillas, 42, **43**

Multicooker Ravioli Lasagna Soup, **44**, 45

Oven-Baked Beef Tacos, 46, **47**

Beef Tacos, Oven-Baked, 46, **47**

Bell peppers

Air Fryer Stuffed Peppers, 178, **179**

BBQ Sloppy Joes, 30, **31**

Breakfast Potatoes, **180**, 181

Cashew Chicken Skillet Stir-Fry, 60, **61**

Ground Beef Quesadillas, 42, **43**

Multicooker Ground Turkey Teriyaki Rice Bowls, 144–45, **145**

Multicooker Ravioli Lasagna Soup, **44**, 45

Pizza Skillet Pasta, 112, **113**

Sheet-Pan Shrimp Fajitas, **134**, 135

Szechuan Pork and Noodles, **114**, 115

Tortellini Pasta Salad, **174**, 175

Tropical Teriyaki Turkey Burgers, **152**, 153

Berry Salad, Citrus, 166, **167**

Blackberries

Citrus Berry Salad, 166, **167**

Piña Colada Fruit Salad, 171, **172**

Blueberries

Lemon Blueberry Trifle, 206, **207**

Piña Colada Fruit Salad, 171, **172**

Braided Pizza Loaf, **98**, 99

Breads

Cheesy Garlic Bread, 158, **159**

Easy Naan, **160**, 161

Easy Parmesan Crescent Rolls, 162, **163**

Twisted Cheese Breadsticks, **164**, 165

Breadsticks, Twisted Cheese, **164**, 165

Breakfast Potatoes, **180**, 181

Broccoli

Cashew Chicken Skillet Stir-Fry, 60, **61**

Multicooker Ground Turkey Teriyaki Rice Bowls, 144–45, **145**

Super Greens, **196**, 197

Szechuan Pork and Noodles, **114**, 115

Broccoli, Air Fryer Parmesan, **176**, 177

Brownies, Lemon, with Lemon Frosting, 208–9, **209**

Bruschetta, Zucchini Feta, 12, **13**

Brussels Sprouts, Garlic Roasted, **190**, 191

Buffalo Chicken Wings, Air Fryer, **50**, 51

Buffalo Ranch Deviled Eggs, 6, **7**

Burgers, Classic, 34, **35**

Burgers, Grilled Teriyaki, **40**, 41

Burgers, Tropical Teriyaki Turkey, **152**, 153

Burritos, Crispy Bean and Cheese, **78**, 79

Burritos, Seven-Layer Dip, 84, **85**

Butter Chicken, Multicooker, **68**, 69

C

Cajun Pasta, Fresh, **82**, 83

Cake Mix Peanut Butter Bars, **200**, 201

Carrots

Cashew Chicken Skillet Stir-Fry, 60, **61**

Easy Sausage Tortellini Soup, **100**, 101

Multicooker Ground Turkey Teriyaki Rice Bowls, 144–45, **145**

Quick Italian Turkey Soup, **146**, 147

Tomato Macaroni Soup, 150, **151**

Tuscan White Bean Soup, 116, **117**

Cashew Chicken Skillet Stir-Fry, 60, **61**

Cheddar cheese

Air Fryer Stuffed Peppers, 178, **179**

Bacon Ranch Chicken, **54**, 55

Baked Ham and Cheese Croissant Sandwiches, 96, **97**

Classic Burgers, 34, **35**

Million-Dollar Dip, **16**, 17

Multicooker Loaded Mac and Cheese,, 108, **109**

Oven-Baked Beef Tacos, 46, **47**

Pizza Skillet Pasta, 112, **113**

Seven-Layer Dip Burritos, 84, **85**

Warm Bacon Cheese Dip, **22**, 23

White Cheddar Corn Chowder, 74, **75**

White Cheddar Shells and Cheese, 90, **91**

Cheese. *See* Cheddar cheese; Colby Jack cheese; Cream cheese; Feta cheese; Monterey Jack cheese; Mozzarella cheese; Parmesan cheese; Swiss cheese

Cheese Breadsticks, Twisted, **164**, 165

Cheese Sandwich, Chopped, **32**, 33

Cheesy Garlic Bread, 158, **159**

Chewy Homemade M&M's Cookies, 202, **203**

Chicken, Bacon Ranch, **54**, 55

Chicken and Pineapple Quesadillas, BBQ, **58**, 59

INDEX

Chicken Bacon Alfredo French Bread
    Pizza, **62**, 63
Chicken dishes, 49–75
    Air Fryer Buffalo Chicken Wings,
        50, 51
    Air Fryer Chicken Tenders, 52, **53**
    Bacon Ranch Chicken, **54**, 55
    Baked Creamy Chicken Taquitos,
        56, **57**
    BBQ Chicken and Pineapple Quesa-
        dillas, **58**, 59
    Cashew Chicken Skillet Stir-Fry,
        60, **61**
    Chicken Bacon Alfredo French
        Bread Pizza, **62**, 63
    Chicken Taco Roll-Ups, 8, **9**
    Mexican Street Corn Chicken Tacos,
        64–65, **65**
    Multicooker Apricot Chicken, **66**, 67
    Multicooker Butter Chicken, **68**, 69
    Perfect Air Fryer Chicken Breasts,
        70, **71**
    Tuscan Pasta, **72**, 73
    White Cheddar Corn Chowder, 74,
        75
Chicken Taco Roll-Ups, 8, **9**
Chicken Tacos, Mexican Street Corn,
    64–65, **65**
Chicken Taquitos, Baked Creamy, 56,
    57
Chicken Tenders, Air Fryer, 52, **53**
Chicken Wings, Air Fryer Buffalo, **50**,
    51
Chili, Multicooker Ground Turkey Taco,
    142, 143
Chopped Cheese Sandwich, **32**, 33
Chowder, New England Clam, 128, **129**
Chowder, White Cheddar Corn, 74, **75**

Cinnamon Sugar Pretzels, White Choc-
    olate, **222**, 223
Cinnamon Twists, **204**, 205
Citrus Berry Salad, 166, **167**
Clam Chowder, New England, 128, **129**
Classic Burgers, 34, **35**
Clementine oranges
    Citrus Berry Salad, 166, **167**
    Piña Colada Fruit Salad, 171, **172**
Coconut Shrimp, Air Fryer, **120**, 121
Colby Jack cheese, Tex-Mex Turkey
    and Rice Skillet, 148, **149**
Cookies, Chewy Homemade M&M's,
    202, **203**
Cookies, Lemon Cheesecake Pudding,
    210, 211
Cookies, PB&J Thumbprint, **214**, 215
Cookies, Red Velvet Whoopie Pie
    Sandwich, **218**, 219
Corn
    Corn Salsa, 182, **183**
    Fiesta Ground Beef Enchiladas, **38**,
        39
    Mexican Street Corn Chicken Tacos,
        64–65, **65**
    Multicooker Ground Turkey Taco
        Chili, **142**, 143
    Tex-Mex Turkey and Rice Skillet,
        148, **149**
    White Cheddar Corn Chowder, 74,
        75
Corn Chowder, White Cheddar, 74, **75**
Corn Salsa, 182, **183**
Cowboy Baked Beans, **184**, 185
Cream cheese
    Bacon Ranch Chicken, **54**, 55
    Baked Creamy Chicken Taquitos,
        56, **57**

Baked Ham and Cheese Croissant
    Sandwiches, 96, **97**
Chicken Taco Roll-Ups, 8, **9**
Fettuccine Alfredo, 80, **81**
Grape Salad, **168**, 169
Million-Dollar Dip, **16**, 17
Multicooker Loaded Mac and
    Cheese, 108, **109**
Multicooker Spinach Artichoke Dip,
    18, **19**
Tuscan Pasta, **72**, 73
Warm Bacon Cheese Dip, **22**, 23
Creamy BBQ Sauce, Crispy Zucchini
    Fries with, 186, **187**
Creamy Beef and Tomato Pasta, 36, **37**
Crescent Rolls, Easy Parmesan, 162,
    163
Crispy Bean and Cheese Burritos, **78**,
    79
Crispy Zucchini Fries with Creamy
    BBQ Sauce, 186, **187**
Croissant Sandwiches, Baked Ham and
    Cheese, 96, **97**
Cube Steak, Air Fryer, with Gravy,
    26–27, **27**
Cucumbers
    Multicooker Salmon Bowls, 126–27,
        127
    Tortellini Pasta Salad, **174**, 175

D

Desserts, 199–223
    Cake Mix Peanut Butter Bars, **200**,
        201
    Chewy Homemade M&M's Cookies,
        202, **203**
    Cinnamon Twists, **204**, 205
    Lemon Blueberry Trifle, 206, **207**

Lemon Brownies with Lemon Frosting, 208–9, **209**

Lemon Cheesecake Pudding Cookies, **210**, 211

Mango Pineapple Frozen Whip, 212, **213**

PB&J Thumbprint Cookies, **214**, 215

Puff Pastry Donuts, 216, **217**

Red Velvet Whoopie Pie Sandwich Cookies, **218**, 219

S'mores Clusters, 220, **221**

White Chocolate Cinnamon Sugar Pretzels, **222**, 223

Deviled Eggs, Buffalo Ranch, 6, **7**

Donuts, Puff Pastry, 216, **217**

E

Easy Naan, **160**, 161

Easy Parmesan Crescent Rolls, 162, **163**

Easy Sausage Tortellini Soup, **100**, 101

Egg Roll in a Bowl, **138**, 139

Eggs, Buffalo Ranch Deviled, 6, **7**

Enchiladas, Fiesta Ground Beef, **38**, 39

Enchiladas, Turkey, 154, **155**

F

Fajitas, Sheet-Pan Shrimp, **134**, 135

Feta cheese

Buffalo Ranch Deviled Eggs, 6, **7**

Citrus Berry Salad, 166, **167**

Green Goddess Vegetable Dip, **14**, 15

Mexican Street Corn Chicken Tacos, 64–65, **65**

Multicooker Salmon Bowls, 126–27, **127**

Tortellini Pasta Salad, **174**, 175

Zucchini Feta Bruschetta, 12, **13**

Fettuccine Alfredo, 80, **81**

Fiesta Ground Beef Enchiladas, **38**, 39

Fish. *See* Seafood dishes

Fish Sticks, Parmesan, with Tartar Sauce, 132–33, **133**

French Bread Pizza, Chicken Bacon Alfredo, **62**, 63

Fresh Cajun Pasta, **82**, 83

Frozen Whip, Mango Pineapple, 212, **213**

Fruit Salad, Piña Colada, 171, **172**

G

Garlic Bread, Cheesy, 158, **159**

Garlic Lime Pork Chops, 102, **103**

Garlic Parmesan Mashed Potatoes, 188, **189**

Garlic Roasted Brussels Sprouts, **190**, 191

Grapes

Grape Salad, **168**, 169

Piña Colada Fruit Salad, 171, **172**

Grape Salad, **168**, 169

Gravy, Air Fryer Cube Steak with, 26–27, **27**

Green chiles

Air Fryer Stuffed Peppers, 178, **179**

Multicooker Ground Turkey Taco Chili, **142**, 143

Queso Blanco Dip, **20**, 21

Tex-Mex Turkey and Rice Skillet, 148, **149**

Turkey Enchiladas, 154, **155**

White Cheddar Corn Chowder, 74, **75**

Green Goddess Vegetable Dip, **14**, 15

Grilled Honey Mustard Pork Chops, **104**, 105

Grilled Teriyaki Burgers, **40**, 41

Ground beef

BBQ Sloppy Joes, 30, **31**

Chopped Cheese Sandwich, **32**, 33

Classic Burgers, 34, **35**

Cowboy Baked Beans, **184**, 185

Creamy Beef and Tomato Pasta, 36, **37**

Grilled Teriyaki Burgers, **40**, 41

Ground Beef Quesadillas, 42, **43**

Multicooker Ravioli Lasagna Soup, **44**, 45

Oven-Baked Beef Tacos, 46, **47**

Ground Beef Enchiladas, Fiesta, **38**, 39

Ground Beef Quesadillas, 42, **43**

Ground turkey

Air Fryer Stuffed Peppers, 178, **179**

Egg Roll in a Bowl, **138**, 139

Honey Garlic Glazed Turkey Meatballs, 140, **141**

Multicooker Ground Turkey Taco Chili, **142**, 143

Multicooker Ground Turkey Teriyaki Rice Bowls, 144–45, **145**

Quick Italian Turkey Soup, **146**, 147

Tex-Mex Turkey and Rice Skillet, 148, **149**

Tomato Macaroni Soup, 150, **151**

Tropical Teriyaki Turkey Burgers, **152**, 153

Ground Turkey Taco Chili, Multicooker, **142**, 143

Ground Turkey Teriyaki Rice Bowls, Multicooker, 144–45, **145**

Guacamole

Oven-Baked Beef Tacos, 46, **47**

Seven-Layer Dip Burritos, 84, **85**

H

Ham
  Baked Ham and Cheese Croissant Sandwiches, 96, **97**
  Pineapple Pasta Skillet, **110**, 111
Ham and Cheese Croissant Sandwiches, Baked, 96, **97**
Honey Garlic Glazed Turkey Meatballs, 140, **141**
Honey Mustard Pork Chops, Grilled, **104**, 105
Hot Italian Trio Sandwiches, **106**, 107

I

Italian Trio Sandwiches, Hot, **106**, 107
Italian Turkey Soup, Quick, **146**, 147

J

Jalapeño peppers
  BBQ Chicken and Pineapple Quesadillas, **58**, 59
  Corn Salsa, 182, **183**
  Mexican Street Corn Chicken Tacos, 64–65, **65**
  Pineapple Mango Salsa, 192, **193**
  Queso Blanco Dip, **20**, 21

K

Kale
  Super Greens, **196**, 197
  Tuscan White Bean Soup, 116, **117**

L

Lasagna Soup, Multicooker Ravioli, **44**, 45
Lemon Blueberry Trifle, 206, **207**
Lemon Brownies with Lemon Frosting, 208–9, **209**
Lemon Cheesecake Pudding Cookies, **210**, 211

Lemon Garlic Shrimp Pasta, **124**, 125
Lettuce
  Hot Italian Trio Sandwiches, **106**, 107
  Oven-Baked Beef Tacos, 46, **47**
  Seven-Layer Dip Burritos, 84, **85**
Loaded Mac and Cheese, Multicooker, 108, **109**

M

M&M's Cookies, Chewy Homemade, 202, **203**
Mac and Cheese, Multicooker Loaded, 108, **109**
Macaroni Soup, Tomato, 150, **151**
Mahi-Mahi, Pan-Seared, **130**, 131
Mangoes
  Mango Pineapple Frozen Whip, 212, **213**
  Pineapple Mango Salsa, 192, **193**
Mango Pineapple Frozen Whip, 212, **213**
Mango Salsa, Pineapple, 192, **193**
Marshmallows
  Orange Cream Yogurt Salad, 170, **171**
  S'mores Clusters, 220, **221**
Mashed Potatoes, Garlic Parmesan, 188, **189**
Meatless dishes, 77–91
  Crispy Bean and Cheese Burritos, **78**, 79
  Fettuccine Alfredo, 80, **81**
  Fresh Cajun Pasta, **82**, 83
  Seven-Layer Dip Burritos, 84, **85**
  Sheet-Pan Pancakes, 86, **87**
  Spinach and Tomato Tortellini, 88, **89**
  White Cheddar Shells and Cheese, 90, **91**

Mexican Street Corn Chicken Tacos, 64–65, **65**
Million-Dollar Dip, **16**, 17
Monterey Jack cheese
  BBQ Chicken and Pineapple Quesadillas, **58**, 59
  Turkey Enchiladas, 154, **155**
Mozzarella cheese
  Air Fryer Parmesan Spinach Stuffed Mushrooms, 2, **3**
  Air Fryer Pizzas, **94**, 95
  Braided Pizza Loaf, **98**, 99
  Cheesy Garlic Bread, 158, **159**
  Chicken Bacon Alfredo French Bread Pizza, **62**, 63
  Fresh Cajun Pasta, **82**, 83
  Hot Italian Trio Sandwiches, **106**, 107
  Multicooker Spinach Artichoke Dip, 18, **19**
  Pineapple Pasta Skillet, **110**, 111
  Pizza Skillet Pasta, 112, **113**
  Twisted Cheese Breadsticks, **164**, 165
Multicooker Apricot Chicken, **66**, 67
Multicooker Butter Chicken, **68**, 69
Multicooker Ground Turkey Taco Chili, **142**, 143
Multicooker Ground Turkey Teriyaki Rice Bowls, 144–45, **145**
Multicooker Loaded Mac and Cheese, , 108, **109**
Multicooker Ravioli Lasagna Soup, **44**, 45
Multicooker Salmon Bowls, 126–27, **127**
Multicooker Spinach Artichoke Dip, 18, **19**

Mushrooms
Air Fryer Parmesan Spinach Stuffed Mushrooms, 2, **3**
Asian-Inspired Beef and Snow Peas, **28**, 29
Pizza Skillet Pasta, 112, **113**
Mushrooms, Air Fryer Parmesan Spinach Stuffed, 2, **3**

N
Naan, Easy, **160**, 161
New England Clam Chowder, 128, **129**

O
Olives
Multicooker Salmon Bowls, 126–27, **127**
Oven-Baked Beef Tacos, 46, **47**
Pizza Skillet Pasta, 112, **113**
Seven-Layer Dip Burritos, 84, **85**
Tortellini Pasta Salad, **174**, 175
Orange Cream Yogurt Salad, 170, **171**
Oranges
Citrus Berry Salad, 166, **167**
Orange Cream Yogurt Salad, 170, **171**
Piña Colada Fruit Salad, 171, **172**
Oven-Baked Beef Tacos, 46, **47**

P
Pancakes, Sheet-Pan, **86**, 87
Pan-Seared Mahi-Mahi, **130**, 131
Parmesan Broccoli, Air Fryer, **176**, 177
Parmesan cheese
Air Fryer Chicken Tenders, 52, **53**
Air Fryer Parmesan Broccoli, **176**, 177
Air Fryer Parmesan Spinach Stuffed Mushrooms, 2, **3**
Air Fryer Pizzas, **94**, 95

Braided Pizza Loaf, **98**, 99
Chicken Bacon Alfredo French Bread Pizza, **62**, 63
Creamy Beef and Tomato Pasta, 36, **37**
Crispy Zucchini Fries with Creamy BBQ Sauce, 186, **187**
Easy Parmesan Crescent Rolls, 162, **163**
Fettuccine Alfredo, 80, **81**
Fresh Cajun Pasta, **82**, 83
Garlic Parmesan Mashed Potatoes, 188, **189**
Hot Italian Trio Sandwiches, **106**, 107
Lemon Garlic Shrimp Pasta, **124**, 125
Multicooker Spinach Artichoke Dip, 18, **19**
Parmesan Fish Sticks with Tartar Sauce, 132–33, **133**
Pizza Skillet Pasta, 112, **113**
Roasted Parmesan Sweet Potatoes, 194, **195**
Spinach and Tomato Tortellini, 88, **89**
Tuscan Pasta, **72**, 73
Warm Bacon Cheese Dip, **22**, 23
White Cheddar Shells and Cheese, 90, **91**
Parmesan Broccoli, Air Fryer, **176**, 177
Parmesan Crescent Rolls, Easy, 162, **163**
Parmesan Fish Sticks with Tartar Sauce, 132–33, **133**
Parmesan Spinach Stuffed Mushrooms, Air Fryer, 2, **3**
Parmesan Sweet Potatoes, Roasted, 194, **195**

Pasta
Creamy Beef and Tomato Pasta, 36, **37**
Easy Sausage Tortellini Soup, **100**, 101
Fettuccine Alfredo, 80, **81**
Fresh Cajun Pasta, **82**, 83
Lemon Garlic Shrimp Pasta, **124**, 125
Multicooker Loaded Mac and Cheese, 108, **109**
Pineapple Pasta Skillet, **110**, 111
Pizza Skillet Pasta, 112, **113**
Quick Italian Turkey Soup, **146**, 147
Spinach and Tomato Tortellini, 88, **89**
Szechuan Pork and Noodles, **114**, 115
Tomato Macaroni Soup, 150, **151**
Tortellini Pasta Salad, **174**, 175
Tuscan Pasta, **72**, 73
White Cheddar Shells and Cheese, 90, **91**
Pasta Salad, Tortellini, **174**, 175
PB&J Thumbprint Cookies, **214**, 215
Peanut Butter Bars, Cake Mix, **200**, 201
Peas
Asian-Inspired Beef and Snow Peas, **28**, 29
Cashew Chicken Skillet Stir-Fry, 60, **61**
Pepperoni
Air Fryer Pizzas, **94**, 95
Braided Pizza Loaf, **98**, 99
Pizza Skillet Pasta, 112, **113**
Perfect Air Fryer Chicken Breasts, 70, **71**
Piña Colada Fruit Salad, 171, **172**

Pineapple
   BBQ Chicken and Pineapple Quesa-
      dillas, **58**, 59
   Grilled Teriyaki Burgers, **40**, 41
   Mango Pineapple Frozen Whip, 212,
      213
   Orange Cream Yogurt Salad, 170,
      171
   Piña Colada Fruit Salad, 171, **172**
   Pineapple Mango Salsa, 192, **193**
   Pineapple Pasta Skillet, **110**, 111
   Tropical Teriyaki Turkey Burgers,
      152, 153
Pineapple Mango Salsa, 192, **193**
Pineapple Pasta Skillet, **110**, 111
Pizza, Chicken Bacon Alfredo French
   Bread, **62**, 63
Pizza Loaf, Braided, **98**, 99
Pizzas, Air Fryer, **94**, 95
Pizza Skillet Pasta, 112, **113**
Pork and Noodles, Szechuan, **114**, 115
Pork Chops, Garlic Lime, 102, **103**
Pork Chops, Grilled Honey Mustard
   Pork Chops, **104**, 105
Pork dishes, 93–117
   Air Fryer Pizzas, **94**, 95
   Baked Ham and Cheese Croissant
      Sandwiches, 96, **97**
   Braided Pizza Loaf, **98**, 99
   Easy Sausage Tortellini Soup, **100**,
      101
   Garlic Lime Pork Chops, 102, **103**
   Grilled Honey Mustard Pork Chops,
      104, 105
   Hot Italian Trio Sandwiches, **106**, 107
   Multicooker Loaded Mac and
      Cheese, 108, **109**
   Pineapple Pasta Skillet, **110**, 111
   Pizza Skillet Pasta, 112, **113**

Szechuan Pork and Noodles, **114**, 115
Tuscan White Bean Soup, 116, **117**
Potatoes
   Bacon-Wrapped Tater Tots with
      Dipping Sauce, **4**, 5
   Breakfast Potatoes, **180**, 181
   Garlic Parmesan Mashed Potatoes,
      188, **189**
   New England Clam Chowder, 128,
      129
Pretzel Bites, Twisted, **10**, 11
Pretzels, White Chocolate Cinnamon
   Sugar, **222**, 223
Puff pastry
   Puff Pastry Donuts, 216, **217**
   Twisted Cheese Breadsticks, **164**,
      165
Puff Pastry Donuts, 216, **217**

Q
Quesadillas, BBQ Chicken and Pineap-
   ple, **58**, 59
Quesadillas, Ground Beef, 42, **43**
Queso Blanco Dip, **20**, 21
Quick Italian Turkey Soup, **146**, 147

R
Ranch Chicken, Bacon, **54**, 55
Raspberries
   Citrus Berry Salad, 166, **167**
   Piña Colada Fruit Salad, 171, **172**
Ravioli Lasagna Soup, Multicooker, **44**,
   45
Red Velvet Whoopie Pie Sandwich
   Cookies, **218**, 219
Refried beans
   Multicooker Ground Turkey Taco
      Chili, **142**, 143
   Seven-Layer Dip Burritos, **84**, **85**

Rice
   Air Fryer Stuffed Peppers, 178, **179**
   Asian-Inspired Beef and Snow Peas,
      28, 29
   Crispy Bean and Cheese Burritos,
      78, 79
   Multicooker Ground Turkey Teriyaki
      Rice Bowls, 144–45, **145**
   Tex-Mex Turkey and Rice Skillet,
      148, **149**
Rice Bowls, Multicooker Ground Tur-
   key Teriyaki, 144–45, **145**
Roasted Parmesan Sweet Potatoes,
   194, **195**
Roll-Ups, Chicken Taco, 8, **9**

S
Salads
   Citrus Berry Salad, 166, **167**
   Grape Salad, **168**, 169
   Orange Cream Yogurt Salad, 170,
      171
   Piña Colada Fruit Salad, 171, **172**
   Tortellini Pasta Salad, **174**, 175
Salmon, Baked, 122, **123**
Salmon Bowls, Multicooker, 126–27,
   127
Salsa, Corn, 182, **183**
Salsa, Pineapple Mango, 192, **193**
Sandwich Cookies, Red Velvet Whoop-
   ie Pie, **218**, 219
Sandwiches, Baked Ham and Cheese
   Croissant, 96, **97**
Sandwiches, Hot Italian Trio, **106**, 107
Sausage
   Easy Sausage Tortellini Soup, **100**,
      101
   Pizza Skillet Pasta, 112, **113**
   Tuscan White Bean Soup, 116, **117**

Sausage Tortellini Soup, Easy, **100**, 101
Seafood dishes, 119–35
    Air Fryer Coconut Shrimp, **120**, 121
    Baked Salmon, 122, **123**
    Lemon Garlic Shrimp Pasta, **124**, 125
    Multicooker Salmon Bowls, 126–27, **127**
    New England Clam Chowder, 128, **129**
    Pan-Seared Mahi-Mahi, **130**, 131
    Parmesan Fish Sticks with Tartar Sauce, 132–33, **133**
    Sheet-Pan Shrimp Fajitas, **134**, 135
Seven-Layer Dip Burritos, 84, **85**
Sheet-Pan Pancakes, **86**, 87
Sheet-Pan Shrimp Fajitas, **134**, 135
Shells and Cheese, White Cheddar, 90, **91**
Shredded turkey, Turkey Enchiladas, 154, **155**
    Air Fryer Coconut Shrimp, **120**, 121
    Lemon Garlic Shrimp Pasta, **124**, 125
    Sheet-Pan Shrimp Fajitas, **134**, 135
Shrimp, Air Fryer Coconut, **120**, 121
Shrimp Fajitas, Sheet-Pan, **134**, 135
Shrimp Pasta, Lemon Garlic, **124**, 125
Side dishes, 157–97
    Air Fryer Parmesan Broccoli, **176**, 177
    Air Fryer Stuffed Peppers, 178, **179**
    Breakfast Potatoes, **180**, 181
    Cheesy Garlic Bread, 158, **159**
    Citrus Berry Salad, 166, **167**
    Corn Salsa, 182, **183**
    Cowboy Baked Beans, **184**, 185
    Crispy Zucchini Fries with Creamy BBQ Sauce, 186, **187**
    Easy Naan, **160**, 161
    Easy Parmesan Crescent Rolls, 162, 163
    Garlic Parmesan Mashed Potatoes, 188, **189**
    Garlic Roasted Brussels Sprouts, **190**, 191
    Grape Salad, **168**, 169
    Orange Cream Yogurt Salad, 170, **171**
    Piña Colada Fruit Salad, 171, **172**
    Pineapple Mango Salsa, 192, **193**
    Roasted Parmesan Sweet Potatoes, 194, **195**
    Super Greens, **196**, 197
    Tortellini Pasta Salad, **174**, 175
    Twisted Cheese Breadsticks, **164**, 165
Skillet Stir-Fry, Cashew Chicken, 60, **61**
Sloppy Joes, BBQ, 30, **31**
S'mores Clusters, 220, **221**
Snow Peas, Asian-Inspired Beef and, **28**, 29
Soup, Multicooker Ravioli Lasagna, **44**, 45
Soup, Tomato Macaroni, 150, **151**
Soup, Tuscan White Bean, 116, **117**
Spinach
    Air Fryer Parmesan Spinach Stuffed Mushrooms, 2, **3**
    Citrus Berry Salad, 166, **167**
    Easy Sausage Tortellini Soup, **100**, 101
    Multicooker Spinach Artichoke Dip, 18, **19**
    Quick Italian Turkey Soup, **146**, 147
    Spinach and Tomato Tortellini, 88, **89**
Spinach and Tomato Tortellini, 88, **89**
Spinach Artichoke Dip, Multicooker, 18, **19**
Spinach Stuffed Mushrooms, Air Fryer Parmesan, 2, **3**
Stir-Fry, Cashew Chicken Skillet, 60, **61**
Strawberries
    Citrus Berry Salad, 166, **167**
    Piña Colada Fruit Salad, 171, **172**
Stuffed Mushrooms, Air Fryer Parmesan Spinach, 2, **3**
Stuffed Peppers, Air Fryer, 178, **179**
Super Greens, **196**, 197
Sweet Potatoes, Roasted Parmesan, 194, **195**
Swiss cheese, Tropical Teriyaki Turkey Burgers, **152**, 153
Szechuan Pork and Noodles, **114**, 115

T
Taco Chili, Multicooker Ground Turkey, **142**, 143
Taco Roll-Ups, Chicken, 8, **9**
Tacos, Mexican Street Corn Chicken, 64–65, **65**
Taquitos, Baked Creamy Chicken, 56, **57**
Tartar Sauce, Parmesan Fish Sticks with, 132–33, **133**
Tater Tots with Dipping Sauce, Bacon-Wrapped, **4**, 5
Teriyaki Burgers, Grilled, **42**, 43
Teriyaki Rice Bowls, Multicooker Ground Turkey, 144–45, **145**
Tex-Mex Turkey and Rice Skillet, 148, **149**
Thumbprint Cookies, PB&J, **214**, 215

Tomatoes
    Air Fryer Stuffed Peppers, 178, **179**
    Chicken Bacon Alfredo French
        Bread Pizza, **62**, 63
    Creamy Beef and Tomato Pasta, 36,
        37
    Easy Sausage Tortellini Soup, **100**,
        101
    Fresh Cajun Pasta, **82**, 83
    Hot Italian Trio Sandwiches, **106**, 107
    Multicooker Ground Turkey Taco
        Chili, **142**, 143
    Multicooker Ravioli Lasagna Soup,
        44, 45
    Multicooker Salmon Bowls, 126–27,
        127
    Oven-Baked Beef Tacos, 46, **47**
    Pineapple Mango Salsa, 192, **193**
    Quick Italian Turkey Soup, **146**, 147
    Seven-Layer Dip Burritos, 84, **85**
    Spinach and Tomato Tortellini, 88,
        89
    Tex-Mex Turkey and Rice Skillet,
        148, **149**
    Tomato Macaroni Soup, 150, **151**
    Tortellini Pasta Salad, **174**, 175
    Tuscan Pasta, **72**, 73
    White Cheddar Corn Chowder, 74,
        75
Tomato Macaroni Soup, 150, **151**
Tortellini, Spinach and Tomato, 88, **89**
Tortellini Pasta Salad, **174**, 175
Tortellini Soup, Easy Sausage, **100**, 101
Tortillas
    Baked Creamy Chicken Taquitos,
        56, **57**

    BBQ Chicken and Pineapple Quesa-
        dillas, **58**, 59
    Chicken Taco Roll-Ups, 8, **9**
    Crispy Bean and Cheese Burritos,
        78, 79
    Fiesta Ground Beef Enchiladas, **38**,
        39
    Ground Beef Quesadillas, 42, **43**
    Mexican Street Corn Chicken Tacos,
        64–65, **65**
    Seven-Layer Dip Burritos, 84, **85**
    Sheet-Pan Shrimp Fajitas, **134**, 135
    Turkey Enchiladas, 154, **155**
Trifle, Lemon Blueberry, 206, **207**
Turkey and Rice Skillet, Tex-Mex, 148,
    149
Turkey Burgers, Tropical Teriyaki, **152**,
    153
Turkey dishes, 137–55. *See also* Ground
    turkey
    Egg Roll in a Bowl, **138**, 139
    Honey Garlic Glazed Turkey Meat-
        balls, 140, **141**
    Multicooker Ground Turkey Taco
        Chili, **142**, 143
    Multicooker Ground Turkey Teriyaki
        Rice Bowls, 144–45, **145**
    Quick Italian Turkey Soup, **146**, 147
    Tex-Mex Turkey and Rice Skillet,
        148, **149**
    Tomato Macaroni Soup, 150, **151**
    Tropical Teriyaki Turkey Burgers,
        152, 153
    Turkey Enchiladas, 154, **155**
Turkey Enchiladas, 154, **155**

Turkey Meatballs, Honey Garlic Glazed,
    140, **141**
Turkey Soup, Quick Italian Turkey, **146**,
    147
Tuscan Pasta, **72**, 73
Tuscan White Bean Soup, 116, **117**
Twisted Cheese Breadsticks, **164**, 165
Twisted Pretzel Bites, **10**, 11

V

Vegetable Dip, Green Goddess, **14**, 15
Vegetarian dishes. *See* Meatless dishes

W

Warm Bacon Cheese Dip, **22**, 23
White Bean Soup, Tuscan, 116, **117**
White Cheddar Corn Chowder, 74, **75**
White Cheddar Shells and Cheese, 90,
    91
White Chocolate Cinnamon Sugar
    Pretzels, **222**, 223
Whoopie Pie Sandwich Cookies, Red
    Velvet, **218**, 219

Y

Yogurt Salad, Orange Cream, 170, **171**

Z

Zucchini
    Crispy Zucchini Fries with Creamy
        BBQ Sauce, 186, **187**
    Multicooker Ravioli Lasagna Soup,
        44, 45
    Quick Italian Turkey Soup, **146**, 147
    Zucchini Feta Bruschetta, 12, **13**
Zucchini Feta Bruschetta, 12, **13**
Zucchini Fries, Crispy, with Creamy
    BBQ Sauce, 186, **187**

Acknowledgments

We never imagined we would ever be creating our ELEVENTH cookbook, but here we are! We couldn't have done it without the incredible support of so many people.

First and foremost, we want to thank our amazing families. You are our biggest cheerleaders, our most honest taste-testers, and the reason we fell in love with home-cooked meals in the first place.

To the incredible team working with *Six Sisters' Stuff*, thank you for your dedication and creativity over the years. Maria, Lindsay, Michele, Taylor, Lucy, Bobbi, Andrew, Yvonne, Brecklyn, Kiersty, Regan, Kate—what would we do without you?! From making slow-cooker food look beautiful to answering a million questions and making sure we've got our "stuff" together, your work has made this all possible.

A huge thank you to our readers and online community. Your enthusiasm, feedback, and support over the years have meant everything to us. Whether you've been with us since the beginning or just discovered *Six Sisters' Stuff*, we are so grateful for you. Your messages, comments, and shared photos of our recipes inspire us daily.

To our publisher and editorial team, thank you for taking a chance on six young women and their "family blog" all those years ago. You take our rough ideas and create something amazing for our readers every time, and we feel so lucky to have worked with you for more than a decade.

Finally, to anyone who has ever gathered around the table with loved ones to share a meal: you are the heart of why we do what we do. We hope this book makes dinnertime a little easier, a little more delicious, and a whole lot more enjoyable.

With gratitude,
The Sisters

About the Authors

Photo by Megan Osburn

Six Sisters' Stuff started in 2011 as a way for the sisters to stay in touch after they moved out of their childhood home and started families of their own. Over the last decade, it has grown into one of the top family-friendly recipe websites on the internet. With their focus on simple, approachable meals, they have become a trusted source for millions of people all over the world.